AF471730

Hope For YOU

Testimonies of God's power that will give you hope And a mini-manual on Exorcism

Jack Giles

authorHOUSE®

AuthorHouse™
1663 Liberty Drive
Bloomington, IN 47403
www.authorhouse.com
Phone: 1-800-839-8640

First published by AuthorHouse 10/12/2011

ISBN: 978-1-4670-4276-5 (e)
ISBN: 978-1-4670-4277-2 (sc)

Library of Congress Control Number: 2011917304

Printed in the United States of America

This book is printed on acid-free paper.

Acknowledgements

Relationships with Godly people are a vital part of Christianity. Satisfying achievements in the community of faith are seldom the result of a solo effort. Preparing a book for publication is no exception.

God has graced my life by allowing me to be in relationship with many precious people. Several of these have volunteered to assist in the preparation of this manuscript. Their input and advice in this project has value beyond measure.

I wish to publicly declare my appreciation to my wife Joy, Belinda and Josh Gwinn, Phyllis Chambliss, Rob Dawkins, and Vickie Hatcher. These individuals have assisted with many facets of this endeavor, including an ornery and cankerous computer.

The sweet, Christ-like spirit of these folks has remarkably blessed my life. Their helpfulness to me will absolutely add to their treasure in Heaven.

Introduction

Hopelessness and despair are rampant in our culture. The title of this book is an absolute word from God to every believer who is struggling with these issues. This volume is about God's answer to these dark and disturbing emotions.

History clearly reveals that God has always intervened in the lives of His troubled children. Such interposing activity by God is called a miracle.

This writing contains a precise account of dozens of miracles. These stories are personal testimonies of almost every imaginable kind of need being met by God by our loving God.

Readers who are uncertain about their relationship with God will be clearly enlightened about how to settle this matter. The author's own experience will aid and simplify this process for others.

All believers who are distressed are candidates for a miracle. Indeed, there is hope for everyone. Allow someone's story herein to become a model for your decision.

Follow the courteous wooing of the Holy Spirit. A loving, gentle and mighty God has a miracle for you. The admonitions in this book will usher you into the abundant life that Jesus Christ intended for you to possess.

The section on exorcism is certain to intrigue. It will likely open up new vistas of understanding regarding this normal Biblical activity. This mini-manual has the potential of becoming a divine catalyst that will make you more victorious.

Contents

Acknowledgements v
Introduction vii
Troubled Lady has a Vision 1
Haunted House on Gulf Coast 3
My Greatest Miracle 5
Arterial Blockages Healed 8
Rheumatoid Arthritis Sufferer Healed 9
Lady Awakened from Coma 11
A Miracle Called Whopper 13
Divine Provision for a Pair of Sandals 15
Cutting Toe Nails Averts Devastating Fire 17
God Fixes a Broken Sewer System 18
Hopeless Heart Patient Has Incredible Recovery 20
How a Lady Happened to Get Drunk In the Pastor's Office 22
Why God Gave Ms. Billie a Miracle 23
God Pays a Towing Fee 25
Miracles Need Not Be Understood 27
Tax Money Provided in an Unusual Way 29
Football-Size Tumor Vanishes 30
No Problem Too Big For God 31
Man Healed by Unintentional Touch 32
Runaway Boy Brought Home by Prayer 33
Betty is Set Free from Fear 34
Pastor's Arthritic Hand Healed 35
A Big Miracle in a Big Toe 36

God's Mercy Prevents Suicide 37
A Diamond Reappears 39
Stomach Growth Disappears Overnight 41
Truck Brain Healed 43
Amazing Grace in a Graveyard 44
Sally Testifies of God's Beautiful Intervention: A Witness to God's Power 45
God Answers an Unusual Prayer for Children 46
Two Alcoholics set free at the Same Time 47
Troubled Medical Doctor Receives Miracle 49
Former Green Bay Packer Receives Miracle 51
Evelyn's Eye Miracle 53
God and our Small Problems or Concerns 55
Pastor Healed of Nagging Back Problem 56
Pastor Healed Emotionally in Worship Time 57
Joy Is Healed from Severe Asthma 59
Grandma Myrtle Saved from Fatal Disease 61
Chinese Lion Dog Healed 63
Vernon's Leg Saved from Amputation 65
The Problem with Words like Terminal 66
Small Boy's Prayer Part of Miracle 68
Cervical Cancer Vanquished by Prayer 70
Broken Old Biker Finds Fountain of Youth 72
A Surprising and Beautiful Miracle 75
Sickness Caused by a Spirit 77
Two Miracles at a Mental Facility 80
God Heals Lady Who Lived in a Cage 82
Dark Spirits Incredibly Vanquished 84
Prominent Christian Leader Set Free 86

An Unexpected Evil Assault 87
An Evil Spirit challenges pastor 88
Mom Declares Wall Posters Were Possessed 89
Man Is Delivered from Twelve Demons 90
Windows of the Soul 92
The Cross is a Symbol of Victory 93
An Unusual Manifestation of Darkness 94
Pastor Set Free from Unclean Spirit 95
Porn under the Mattress 96
Haunted House in West Texas 97
Who Was the Stranger? 98
Scott and Tonya Dared to Dream Big! 99
God Works in Mysterious Ways 101
Darlene Shares some Family Miracles 102
Obedience: the Key to God's Blessings 104
The Danger of Saying No to God 106
Black Lab Alerts Couple of Danger 108
A Social Security Miracle 110
Miracle in a Miami Hospital 111
Musings on Exorcism 112
A Few Quirky Experiences to Make You Grin 120
Epilogue 125

Troubled Lady has a Vision

Mary's freedom came only after God gave her a vision. She was thirty years old, attractive, articulate, well educated, but profoundly distraught. She was at her wit's end.

For as long as Mary could remember, she had been overwhelmed by ugly secrets. One of the painful memories she had was her lengthy bondage to masturbation. Intensive professional therapy did not effectively address this problem.

Another manifestation of something deep, dark and vicious suddenly surfaced. She was now besieged by sexual lust that was tormenting and powerful. Defeat, shame and regret were now rampant in her life.

I was relaxing in my recliner on a Sunday night after church. I had removed my shoes and expected absolute privacy after a long but good day at church. The doorbell invaded my peace of mind. "Who could that possibly be?" I mused

After my wife introduced me to our visitor, I led the troubled lady to my office. I listened intently to her tragic story. She had come seventy-five miles because someone had suggested that I might be able to help her. I never knew who sent her.

I take ministry very seriously; but I share in the framework of a structure hammered out through experience. Therefore, there is a routine through which success is normally achieved. I ministered to Mary through my normal manner of procedure and felt that it was successful.

However, for the next four Sunday nights, Mary returned, unannounced. I grew very frustrated, because I was not effective in helping her. After the second Sunday night, I really did not want to see Mary; because I had exhausted my expertise. She was no better off than before we began.

On the lady's last visit, I prayed a very long time. I honestly told God that I could not help her. Pleadingly, I sought His intervention. God was faithful and answered my cry for the helpless lady. As we sat in silence for a long time, Mary began to tell me about the vision that she just had. Her speech was slow and deliberate. Her eyes fairly glowed with awe.

In the vision, Mary saw herself as a six-year-old child clearly being molested. Like a movie screen, the vision revealed that with which her conscious mind could not deal. The graphic, ugly details of the abuse were exposed for the first time. Now, she knew how and why her bondage began.

Mary shared that she felt as if an octopus-like evil being with many long tentacles had held her. As the vision progressed, the tentacles of the evil one began to come off one by one. I continued to pray until she was totally free.

Healing had come to Mary as she realized that an evil deed done by another had initiated her bondage. She realized that she was not an inherently bad person. She was able to forgive and, therefore, be forgiven.

Mary's feet had now been firmly planted on the road to emotional, spiritual, and mental wholeness. God had again shown Himself mighty to deliver. It was all about Jesus Christ and the manifestation of His innovative presence.

We give praise and glory to God for this beautiful miracle. May our faith be enlarged to expect more and more of the mighty acts of God.

Haunted House on Gulf Coast

Realizing that an unseen personality inhabits the house in which you and your family live can be profoundly unsettling. This possibility is a mystery that cannot be fully understood or explained by anyone at this time. This writer is acquainted with several such bizarre accounts.

In most cases known to me, the individuals are articulate, well-educated Christian people. Similar things happen in all houses that are reputed to be haunted. Strange and unexplainable describes what goes on in these houses.

My friend, William, lived in a haunted house. Intermittently, sounds would resonate from his attic, like a heavy-footed person walking around. Interior doors would sometimes close when no air current or person could be involved. A child's ball would occasionally roll, seemingly under its own power. These manifestations produced consternation and anxiety in this family.

The homeowner approached me at a Bible conference and asked my advice on his problem. He requested that I come to his home and help him deal with this phenomenon. I responded that I would share with him how to deal with the situation, and it would not be necessary for me to be there.

It was two months before I saw my friend again. I inquired if he had taken care of the problem that he had shared. He replied that he was waiting until I could be with him. "Fine," I said to William, "let's do it."

The following is the method with which I recommend dealing with these situations. My conviction is that the spiritual head of the home should take the initiative in removing dark spirits from the premises. Hauntings are sometimes the result of violent acts in the history of the domicile, or a material object may give refuge to the troubling spirit.

The spiritual leader of the family should begin by praying for revelations regarding the origin of the paranormal activity on the premises. All suspicious objects should be removed and immediately destroyed. God's under shepherd in the home should go into every room in the house and command in Jesus Name every dark or foul spirit to leave. The house and all its contents, along with the family should now be dedicated to God.

If the attic has walking space, it also should be cleansed by prayer and removing the objects that might be troublesome. The one praying over the house should also walk around the perimeter of the house and land, dedicating the entire property to God.

Any possible familiar spirit can be vanquished in Jesus Name. Familiar spirits can be passed down through generations of family members. These, too, are subject to the Godly authority of the home's spiritual head.

I accompanied William as he went through the process that I had suggested. This experience happened nineteen years ago. Since that time, no paranormal activity has occurred in the house.

My Greatest Miracle

The religious culture in which I was mentored denied the reality of miracles. Consequently, for thirty-five years I neither saw nor expected to encounter a sovereign miracle of God.

Because of the extreme kindness of God, I was delivered from this theological untruth. This came about when I realized that the declaration, "I am the Lord, and I do not change," is really true (Malachi 3:6).

To me, this simply means that He will forever remain the same. Inherent in this is the fact that He will forever do the things that He has always done. Since this veil has been removed from my eyes, I have experienced countless beautiful miracles.

These fascinating acts of God have been expressed in both the physical and material realms of my life. The greatest and most significant work of God in my life, however, was a spiritual matter.

This happened when I was eighteen years of age, and was a life-changing encounter for me. At that time, I chose to receive Jesus Christ as my Savior. I would forever be different in my entire being.

I made no attempt to change anything about my life. However, everything about me did change.

There had been no peace in my life. Now peace became constant in my heart. My thoughts and speech formerly were unclean. Instantly, He cleaned up my speech and began to bring my thoughts under subjection. My hopes and dreams had not been honorable, but now they were.

Before, life had been all about self; after my acceptance of Christ, it was all about Jesus. In the past, focus was on what I wanted for my future. Suddenly, it became what He might want for me.

For the first time, joy began to come into my life. The change was genuine and permanent. When Jesus Christ came into my life, a new and positive beginning was birthed.

I had been religious for many years. My mom and dad were very fine Christian people. Attending church on Sunday and Wednesday nights was routine in our family.

When I was nine or ten years old, a well-meaning minister coerced this very shy child into church membership and baptism. There was no explanation regarding personally receiving Christ into my heart and life.

The following years were a time of personal unrest and emptiness. I was a good church member, but I was not a good person.

My status was simple. I was outwardly very religious, but God was not in my life. Therefore, I could be nothing but unrighteous. I was spiritually a lost person; therefore, meaning and purpose were absent from my life.

It has been said that all people are born with a "hole" in their heart. The only thing that can fill that place is God. I certainly had that "hole." I was ignorant of the fact that I needed to find God.

Because of His passionate love, He sought me! He also wooed me, pursued and apprehended me!

Who was this "He"? Francis Thompson, in a poem written in 1893, called Him the "Hound of Heaven." He describes God as following the fleeing soul in a never ending pursuit. This, my friend, is God's amazing grace.

Before my divine encounter, no one had ever engaged me in conversation about my soul. A young pastor, James Denton Watson, gently and graciously asked me if I had been saved.

I was accompanying him in delivering some children home after worship on a Sunday night. After he heard my "no," to his question, he proceeded to clearly share all that Jesus had done for me on the cross and through His resurrection.

We had this conversation in the front seat of his 1954 Chevrolet. He encouraged me to choose to receive Christ right then and there. The best decision that I ever made then ensued.

I simply admitted the obvious to God; that I was a sinner, but that I wanted to be saved. I acknowledged my understanding that Jesus died on the cross for my sins. I invited Christ to come into my heart, save me and take control of my life.

The peace of God came upon me immediately. I then went and shared with my family about the decision that I had just made.

Zechariah 13:1 says that there was coming a day in which God would open "a fountain for sin and impurity." This prophetic spiritual utterance pointed forward to what Jesus would accomplish through His death and resurrection.

What I could never do, He did in me the moment that I invited Him into my heart. I was indeed cleansed from sin and impurity.

II Corinthians 5:17 says, “If anyone be in Christ, he is a new Creature: old things are passed away; behold all things are become new.” This was my experience.

Almost every human being is religious, but many have never made the decisive choice to ask Jesus Christ to come into their hearts and lives and be their Savior. If you have never made this personal decision, you are encouraged to stop and do it right now.

In a simple and uncomplicated way, talk to God through His Son, Jesus Christ. Just tell Him that you realize that you need Him and then proceed to ask Him to come into your life and save you. He will; please go ahead and pray right now!

You will never regret this decision. Someday you will know that this was the greatest day of your life. I absolutely know that the day that I came to know Christ was my finest hour.

Arterial Blockages Healed

Al had heart problems. He felt that they were getting worse. Over a period of time, the discomfort reached such a level that he sought help from a specialist. The medical conclusion was that one artery was almost totally shut off. Immediately after a heart catherization, a stent was successfully inserted in the most endangered artery.

Al Berg shared in his testimony that his doctor had given him a grim prognosis after the heart catherization was completed. There was an intense concern for two other arteries. One had a seventy percent blockage, and the other had a fifty percent blockage. The attending physicians indicated that open-heart surgery, not stents, would be required to remedy the problem at some point in the future.

I had the privilege to share in the New Life Assembly of God Church in El Paso, Texas, in June, 2010. This was a very special group of people. Magnificent groundwork had been laid for the miracles that happened in those services. Al was one who came for prayer on Sunday night.

I prayed that Al's arteries would be unblocked. He sensed in his heart that he was healed. He rejoiced over this new beginning.

A few weeks later, however, a severe discomfort returned. Naturally, this was cause for great concern. His wife took him to an emergency room because they feared a heart attack might be imminent. The hospital personnel ended up giving him morphine.

The next day, the doctor came by to give Al the test results. "I don't know what your pain was, but it was not your heart," he emphasized. To prove his point, he showed Al a set of "pictures." While the older x-rays clearly showed blockages, the latest images showed, according to the doctor, "virtually no blockage at all, but only a slight narrowing of one of the arteries."

Rheumatoid Arthritis Sufferer Healed

"There is no cure for this disease," the somber family physician announced to the young lady. Her heart was gripped by a fear that was colder than the frigid room in which she shivered. With every heart beat, the words, "no cure" pulsated violently through her brain.

Jennifer's heart cried, "I'm too young for this. That disease is only for old folks, and I'm still in my teens! This is just a nightmare. I'll soon wake up, and this will all be over."

Her wake up was to the fact that her body was being ravaged by a cruel and unrelenting devil of a disease. Rheumatoid arthritis patients are subjected to a level of constant agony that is incomprehensible to most of the population. The next thirty-four years were to be a battle to survive for the valiant lady.

Those years often seemed like an eternity to a youth whose life was supposed to be just blossoming. Her joints began to swell and twist and be on fire with pain that seemed beyond survival. Night and day, tears that could not be held back flowed from a broken heart.

Surgical intervention was necessary all too many times during those pain-stained years. Fingers and hip joints were targeted by this crippling disease that would "give no quarter".

Much of Jennifer's life was a trek through the "valley of deep darkness" that is spoken of by King David in Psalm 23:4. Pain, constant companion though it was, was always overshadowed by the Chief Shepherd to whom Jennifer belonged. His grace was always sufficient.

Many times I was privileged to pray for this now fully-adult lady. God gave me perseverance to continue to ask Him to heal her. It should be noted that miracles of healing are seldom accompanied by "thunder and lightning."

Sometime in August of 2009, I received an exciting call from Jennifer. She had gone to her doctor where she was subjected to a battery of tests. Afterward, the doctor came in and declared that there was now no arthritis in her body. The news was so incredible that it had to be repeated in order for Jennifer to internalize this wonderful news.

“Brother Jack,” she said, “the last time that you prayed for me, you asked God to vanquish all arthritis from my body. He now has done that,” she joyfully declared. Several months later, our Lord supernaturally straightened one of her fingers.

As Jennifer shared her story with me, I learned some vital information that was as important as the “prayer of faith.” About the time that I prayed for Jen, she felt the need to forgive an individual that had wronged her. When this was done, faith and forgiveness converged into a divine catalyst that set her free from the power of an evil disease.

Lady Awakened from Coma

The emergency room doctor said, "We can find no reason medically why this lady is in a coma. A trace of marijuana was evident in her blood, but nothing else was found. It certainly would not cause this." With a furrowed brow, the doctor just stood there shaking his head.

For the sake of privacy, we will call this young lady Mona. She was twenty-one years of age. She had been found in this condition by one of her friends the previous night. The early-on diagnosis was that she had over-dosed on something.

This situation was called to the attention of our church secretary midmorning the following day. It was reported that Mona would probably not survive. We were grieved by this tragic news but we, nevertheless, did ask God in Jesus' name to restore her health.

About midafternoon, we received another call concerning Mona. Although my first thought was that she had died, on the contrary, the caller was requesting more prayer for the young lady. With this bit of news, I headed to Rush Foundation's emergency complex. I was immediately escorted to the patient's room.

What I found in this room shocked me. An attractive blond, with an appearance younger than her age, lay very still on a gurney. I had several granddaughters about her age.

A female cousin of the patient stood near the bed sobbing. I immediately began to pray for Mona's healing. This continued for fifteen or twenty minutes, but there was no visible change.

This was the moment that the E. R. physician entered and announced that they could find no medical reason for the patient's problem. After his leaving, I began to think perhaps something demonic might be involved in this crisis.

I inquired of the cousin if Mona might dabble in witchcraft. The lady did not know or would not tell me if she did possess this knowledge. I decided, as an old saying goes, "to take the bull by the horns."

Leaning over the hospital gurney, I verbally canceled all work of witchcraft in Mona's life. I spoke to all curses that had been uttered against her. All this I did in the name of Jesus Christ. With forceful, but not loud speech, I said, "Mona, I command you in the name of Jesus Christ to wake up."

I repeated this command about three times, and immediately Mona became wide-awake. This was absolutely an awesome sight. Upon awakening, Mona wept profusely for a while. I gently encouraged her and spoke blessings on her before leaving.

The surprised E.R. staff soon discharged the miracle patient. The following Wednesday night, Mona attended a class at church and shared what God had done for her. Indeed, there really is nothing too hard for God.

A Miracle Called Whopper

Whopper was a dog, and an incredibly special one as you will discover. Her story is heartwarming, encouraging and inspiring. Jerry Bratu considered this luxurious, petite animal to have been a stabilizing and healing presence in a dark night of his soul.

Bratu found himself struggling in the agonizing and frustrating process of recovery after an accident. Being hobbled by crutches is an acute emotional challenge to one built on a large frame and accustomed to running wide open.

In the midst of Jerry's dark valley, a friend presented him with a gift. The present was an incredibly small puppy that was given an unusual name. In retrospect, this minute creature was an absolute God-send. The benevolent acquaintance was no doubt prompted by the Spirit of God.

The extraction from which Bratu's pet descended is a breed known as the Lhasa apso. Some argue that this strain of dog is the pinnacle of canine creation. They indeed are strikingly beautiful and graceful animals.

Whopper's hair was a splendid, sparkling honey and white sheen. Lhasa apsos seem to have been fashioned by God specifically to become companions for those who are hurting.

Jerry's intriguing little critter was the picture of health for five years. The laughter and joy that resulted from their companionship has often produced a supernatural nostalgia. It was like a daydream that often carried a troubled heart to a far-away land where a boy and his dog were again wonderfully carefree, even if only momentarily.

Jerry and his wife, Liz, were distraught and troubled when they realized that Whopper was a very sick dog. Her magnificent coat began to disintegrate. A miserable itch then seized their four-legged family member.

For three years, two Veterinarians compassionately used their skills endeavoring to bring wellness again to Whopper. Finally, the family was presented with very undesirable options in regard to their beloved pet.

Their choice canine could be taken to the School of Veterinary Science at Mississippi State University or mercifully put down.

The Bratus had lovingly and willingly spent a great deal of money during those long and painful three years. They simply could not afford the Starkville gamble. With hearts heavier than they could articulate, they knew deep down that there had to be a better way than euthanasia.

One afternoon in my office, Jerry shared with me what seemed to be a grievous reality. Whopper, because of her misery, had remained in his old ugly truck. I am convinced that a Holy Spirit thought was suddenly birthed in my brain. It was simply, "Jerry, why don't we go out and pray for Whopper?" There was no flash of lightning or drum rolls of thunder, but an infinitely loving and merciful God made Whopper well right then and there.

God gave Jerry and Whopper Bratu five good years after that magnificent miracle. After having incredibly fulfilled her purpose, Whopper, unexpectedly one afternoon, slipped through the veil into the presence of God.

Whopper's abrupt departure was, indeed, a heartbreaking experience. However, just as God had healed their pet, He also restored the joy of the Lord to Liz and Jerry. The mention of the name "Whopper" never fails to evoke a huge smile from this couple.

Remembering a miracle called Whopper, Psalms 150:1-2&6 becomes like a neon sign in my heart:

Praise the Lord!
Praise God in His sanctuary;
Praise Him in His mighty
Expanse.

Praise Him for His mighty
Deeds;
Praise Him according to His
Excellent greatness.

Let everything that hath breath
Praise the Lord.

Praise Ye the Lord!

Divine Provision for a Pair of Sandals

God is awesome. He meets needs both great and small for His beloved children. One of the small, but unusual needs that He met for me took place in Destin, Florida.

We were in this beautiful town for a wonderful occasion. Our adopted grandson, Joshua, and his fiancée, Katie, had chosen this exquisite spot for their marriage ceremony. The time was early October 2009. The weather could not have been lovelier for the beach wedding.

The rehearsal was on a Friday night. Everything was exciting and happy on this occasion except my feet. All in attendance were either barefooted or wearing sandals. This was an unwelcome realization for me.

Obviously, my ancient bare feet did not tolerate this beach very well. Actually, they screamed at every small pebble on which they accidentally trod. Somehow, sandals had never been in vogue for this country boy. However, after that evening, my feet demanded that they be given a larger measure of respect.

Early Saturday morning found me prowling the local Super Wal-Mart environs. As a thirsty person in a parched land longs for water, so I sought the shoe department.

With a huge smile, I meandered the seemingly miles of footwear. My smile soon began to fade as it became evident that no sandals would respond to my desperate quest.

An unwitting clerk dashed all human hope that sandals and I might be joined. With a faint and tentative smile, I asked, "Ma'am, where are the sandals?"

Unsympathetically and business-like she informed me, "Sir, we have no sandals in the store."

I felt like I had just been "bonged". I thought, "I'm from the red hills of Mississippi. What do I know about the season for sandals around the sea?"

With a sweeping gesture of her left arm she said, "Let me show you our flip-flops."

I was led to a monstrous rack of stunning pink flip-flops. They looked like they may have been dipped in Pepto-Bismol.

In frustration and despair for my acutely sensitive feet, my heart cried, "Lord, I need some sandals."

In a definitely startled tone of voice, the clerk immediately, declared. "Look." "Here is a pair of sandals."

No one would have been surprised that they were exactly my size. I was able to traipse through the beach wedding with deliriously happy feet. I continue to be amazed at the generosity of my heavenly Father. I will definitely praise Him with all my being all my days.

Cutting Toe Nails Averts Devastating Fire

This story is quite bizarre, yet is an amazing example of God intervening to protect our safety. It is also obvious that God sometimes chooses such unconventional methods that it makes us laugh.

A few weeks ago, in early August, 2010, a major fire was narrowly averted in our home. This sequence of events began late one afternoon after I had worked in the yard for a couple of hours. While dressing after showering, I snagged a sock on a ragged toe-nail. Out of necessity, I sought out my extra large nail clippers.

Sitting on the side of my bed, I thought, "Might as well cut them all while I am at it." Needless to say, I made quite a mess in the process. Also, I thought, "Praise God for Dust Busters to clean up this gruesome sight."

I quickly retrieved our Dust Buster from the utility room. To my dismay this small cleaning wonder would barely pick up the litter that I had caused. After finishing the project, I slid the unit back into the sheath and made a surprising discovery. The light indicating that it was plugged in was not working.

"Well, I guess the thing has finally died," I sadly concluded. I then attempted to unplug the unit from the wall receptacle. To my absolute surprise, the apparatus was so hot that I could hardly touch it.

Not only was the instrument almost red hot, but its entire covering had turned from white to light brown. A fire would have soon erupted had the situation not been discovered.

Given the lateness of the afternoon, the fire could have erupted after we went to sleep. The unit was not more than ten feet from our bedroom door. If a fire had occurred, we could have been trapped inside this room. The conclusion of the matter is that had I not cut my-toe nails, a devastating and tragic fire most likely would have occurred. Further, I am confident that "God causes all things to work together for good to those who love Him, to those who are called according to His purpose," Romans 8:28.

God Fixes a Broken Sewer System

"Cast all your cares upon Him, for He cares for you," Peter exhorts in 1 Peter 5:7. Martin Luther is reputed to have said, "God does nothing except in answer to the prayers of His people." If this is true, then many have surely missed-out on many divine encounters because we simply did not ask.

This truth is verbalized by the Holy Spirit to the Biblical writer James when he penned the words, "We receive not because we ask not." There are many wonderful Christians who never think to pray about things like broken personal property.

Biblical admonishing to pray indicates that the mundane and spiritual alike are important to our Heavenly Father.

Rudolph was an independent insurance agent. He was our new health insurance coverage agent. This young man was an unusually fine Christian. His dad was an outstanding local pastor for many years.

When this event took place, Rudy lived in Philadelphia, Mississippi. He owned a home there. During one of our first consultations, our new friend revealed a rather severe, personal concern. The sewer system at his home had a major problem.

He was really bothered because the projected cost to remedy this situation seemed to be prohibitively high. "Rudy, have you prayed about this situation?" I asked. He admitted that he really had not thought about bringing this matter to God in prayer.

I proceeded to share my conviction that God desires us to bring all our troubles to Him. He promptly agreed that this sounded like good theology to him. After we finished our business that day, I offered to pray with Rudolph about his serious sewer problem.

In very simple language, I laid the pressing and expensive need before God and requested from Him a miracle fix. A couple of weeks later my agent friend shared with me that the problem had suddenly and mysteriously vanished.

Let the reader be encouraged to embrace the truth that many

miraculous manifestations of divine grace await simply the asking. Right now would be a very good time to begin.

Hebrews 4:16 says in part, “Let us fearlessly and confidently and boldly draw near to the throne of grace” (Amplified Bible).

Hopeless Heart Patient Has Incredible Recovery

"Mr. Gregory has substantial and very serious heart disease. I regret to share this bad news with the family," the doctor announced. "Furthermore," he continued, "the patient is too old and too sick to survive bypass surgery. Medical treatment will probably produce a life expectancy of perhaps six months."

James Gregory was 87 years old. Because Jesus Christ was his Lord, he had successfully navigated numerous valleys of deep darkness. The doctor making this prognosis was an incredibly good heart surgeon and a fine Christian gentleman.

The sympathetic physician took all the time necessary to answer every question asked by the family. Jay's loved ones were appreciative of the doctor's kindness and genuine concern.

The following day I had planned to visit Mr. Gregory late in the morning. However, about 7:30 A.M., I felt a strong urgency to go immediately to the hospital. Jay's wife, Estelle, and numerous family members were gathered in the large waiting room at the medical facility.

The heart surgeon and I happened to approach the family at the same time that morning. The ashen-faced doctor declared, "I have very bad news to share with the family. Mr. Gregory must have surgery immediately, or he will die today. His condition has deteriorated to the point that there is absolutely no alternative," he emphasized.

The surgeon continued to speak, "I have already ordered the nurses to begin preparation for the surgery. Unless you tell me to stop the process, we will expedite the matter because he really doesn't have much time otherwise."

After the doctor had dropped this verbal bombshell, everyone seemed stunned. There was a huge vacuum of silence; not a word was spoken. Inside of me, it was as if there was a screaming to pray. "Excuse me, Doctor. I am the pastor, and in view of what you have just shared,

I feel an urgent need to pray for Mr. Gregory and for you," I pleaded. He enthusiastically agreed.

I implored God to bestow mercy and healing grace on Jay Gregory. I asked God to give divine expertise to His servant, the surgeon.

I am sure that many people came before God with similar pleas during the next several hours. Nearly four hours later, the doctor returned wearing a great big smile. He promptly announced, "Well, folks, the surgery was wonderfully successful. Mr. Gregory did surprisingly well, and he is going to be fine."

The atmosphere was sort of like being in church services for a while after that pronouncement. The presence of God was in that waiting room. He also had obviously been in the surgical unit.

It was also incredible that James Gregory was in the cardiac recovery room only one night. He was then transferred to a regular room.

During the nearly two years since that major miracle happened to Jay, his heart has been fine. My friend and brother, James Gregory, continues to be a trophy of sovereign grace.

How a Lady Happened to Get Drunk In the Pastor's Office

I was there. I saw the whole thing. She actually passed out on the floor. I suppose that I was somewhat responsible for things getting out of control. She was "out" for about twenty minutes.

Her name was Virginia. From the time she was able to get up from the floor until she and her husband drove away, the lady was absolutely giddy. She was overwhelmed with the peace and joy of the Lord. It was necessary for her husband, Donald, to be her "crutch" in getting to their vehicle. Virginia had just experienced a divine epiphany.

This experience all began a couple of hours earlier at a tent revival at the Okatibbee Reservoir near Collinsville, Mississippi. The Holy Spirit had moved mightily during the ministry time that Tuesday night.

I was the master of ceremonies for the revival that week. God had wonderfully manifested Himself the first three nights of the tent meeting.

After service that night, the couple approached me and asked if they might talk to me in the church office as soon as possible. A late night meeting was, therefore, necessary. Virginia very gently indicated that she needed a fresh touch from God.

Later in the church office, Virginia cried out in prayer for an infilling of the Holy Spirit. She sat in a chair by her husband. As she prayed, I gently put my hands on her head and prayed that God would answer her heart cry.

Suddenly, Virginia totally relaxed and slid out of her chair on to the carpet. She was "under the influence" of God's sweet presence.

The Bible's Book of Acts, second chapter, records that many people had a similar experience: These first Christians had become "drunk on the Holy Spirit."

Why God Gave Ms. Billie a Miracle

This is a unique and intriguing account of divine grace. Ms. Billie was one of our delightful senior adults. The story unfolds after Billie was admitted to Jeff Anderson Medical Clinic with a case of severe bronchitis.

During her recuperating time, heart abnormalities suddenly surfaced. The heart specialists who were called in were of the opinion that some heart blockage was present in the patient.

A heart catherization was scheduled to clarify the issue. The day before this procedure was performed, a nurse attempted, to no avail, to locate a vein in both of Billie's arms.

A total of fifteen attempts were made to find one of her elusive veins in order to begin the necessary solutions. Both arms were covered with huge ugly blotches where the failures occurred.

The morning of the planned catherization, I observed, in horror, the results of the failed efforts. Billie's doctor had related that a "cut-down" would be done because it was imperative that a vein be located.

The problem did not involve inadequacy on the part of any employee. The issue was a physical thing with the patient. The veins in her arms were very small and had a tendency to "roll" at the approach of a needle. It was, therefore, concluded that a normal procedure was not possible.

I was there to pray with Ms. Billie before the catherization was to begin. Actually, I had already prayed before this scenario unfolded. A medical technician from the lab entered the room and, identifying himself, stated that he was going to make one more attempt to locate a vein.

The tech stated that the doctors really did not want to perform a "cut-down" on Billie. To have missed this divine appointment, I pretty much would have been a back-slider. Because of an inner prompting, I said, "Excuse me, sir; I am the lady's pastor. May I pray for you both right now?"

"That will be fine," was his reply.

I prayed for divine expertise for this gentle-spirited man. I asked for

God's mercy to be lavished on Billie in these difficult moments. About that time more visitors entered the room making it expedient that some of us step out while this procedure was being done.

We had hardly gotten out of the room when the medical tech also came out. He stopped and said to me, "Thanks for the prayer. It worked."

There were several reasons why God gave Ms. Billie this miracle. First, He was bringing glory and honor to Himself. We have often since honored Him for this special display of His grace that day. The second reason for this mighty act was the magnificent love in His heart for this special senior adult.

There were probably several other reasons why God did this beautiful thing for our friend. For time's sake, let it be simply noted that the medical technician, the family and the rest of us needed to see God show up at that precise moment.

God Pays a Towing Fee

"Bro. Jack, me and the kids broke down in heavy traffic. Can you come and help us?" The lady's voice had a hint of panic in it. She continued, "Kirk, her husband, said to call you." The couple had five children and one mode of transportation.

About a zillion thoughts raced through my mind as I processed her request. "Where exactly are you located?" I urgently inquired.

"I'm at the traffic light on College Drive and Highway 19 North," she lamented.

"I'll be there as quickly as possible," I promised.

Actually, I felt powerless to help in this situation. I thought, "I'll just jump in and see what God does to meet this need." My philosophy is that we really should live by the words of Jesus Christ that are often referred to as the Golden Rule.

This Bible verse is found in Matthew 7:12: "However you want people to treat you, so treat them." Living by the Golden Rule does not mean doing what is comfortable, but doing what is right.

The intersection that Ruth mentioned is one of the busiest in the city. The traffic signal where her van stopped was between Meridian Community College and the Mississippi State University Branch Campus on Highway 19.

It only took me ten minutes to arrive at the scene of the problem. A tow truck and two police cars were already on the scene. The officers were directing traffic, while the wrecker hooked up to the frustrated lady's van. I had forgotten that all vehicles breaking down in traffic are immediately removed by order of the police department.

I followed the frazzled mom to the garage where she and her children were towed. Upon arrival, I watched as a mechanic immediately started her vehicle.

Ruth looked at the tow truck driver and said, "I guess I'll have to leave my van here because I do not have enough money to pay your fee."

I then addressed the driver, "Sir, I am this lady's pastor. I will pay the bill, and they can reimburse me whenever."

The driver responded by asking, "You are Brother Giles, aren't you?"

"Yes, sir, I replied somewhat quizzically.

The gentleman continued by saying, "then there will be no charge."

"Thank you very much and God bless you," I emphatically spoke to the generous man. Miracles come in many sizes and in many ways. God had again gotten in the middle of a problem and provided a divine solution.

Miracles Need Not Be Understood

Miracles take place when God intervenes in the affairs of man to meet some need in the human scene. Such acts are beautiful, magnificent and intriguing. In the release of these mysterious and benevolent acts, God uses both people and angels.

Sometimes He utilizes only one of these methods, yet often their activities are intertwined. There are occasions in which angels (messengers of God) take on human form. Indeed, there are times when we never really know if we have encountered a mortal or one of these special messengers.

One such experience happened to me in about 1990. The place was a very lovely mountainous area in southwest North Carolina. The privilege to share in an area church brought my wife and me to this scenic spot.

On Saturday before our arrival, the right back tire of our vehicle had gone flat. The following Monday, I drove to a nearby service station to have the tire repaired. The attendant took one look at the tire and said, "Sir, this tire is ruined. You will have to have a new tire."

"Point me to a tire store," I said to the local pastor. Arriving at the tire store, I made a request. "I need to purchase a tire. I don't want your most expensive tire, nor do I want a cheap one. I want a mid-line priced tire," I stressed to the manager.

After about thirty minutes, the salesman returned to the waiting room and handed me the car keys. "You can drive your car out now," he stated.

"Thank you," I responded, "but I will pay you and then drive the car out of the shop."

The employee jolted me by his response. "There will be no charge," he offered.

"But, sir," I protested, "I did not come in here looking for something for nothing."

The gentleman continued, "There is no charge, and that's final."

After expressing my appreciation for this kindness, I said, "Thank you, Lord, for your grace and mercy." Whether this was solely an act of human kindness, the work of an angel, or a combination of both, I shall never know.

I do know that God in His mercy had intervened to meet our unique need. It is not important that I understand, but it is crucial that I rejoice and give Him glory, honor and praise.

Tax Money Provided in an Unusual Way

Major anxiety always comes when April 15 arrives, and tax money is insufficient. When this prospect is imminent, there are several responses folks can make. Some people just freak out with fear and go ballistic with despair. There are others who file for an extension with the Internal Revenue Service.

There is at least one more excellent way to face such a crisis as this, at least for my wife and me. This better way is to pray. Several years ago, we had a rather remarkable and unusual answer to such a prayer. At that particular time, we owed the I.R.S. about $550.00.

We asked Father God to provide the needed funds. He did so in quite an unexpected way. I was asked to preach a revival to a small and predominately Native American congregation. The people were precious, but the community was economically depressed. The church was about seven hours from where we lived.

When we travel to minister, money is never a factor in such decisions. God is faithful to provide for those who are obedient. During the revival week, offerings were never mentioned, nor were they a concern.

That week I always sat on a front pew, on the right side, facing the pulpit. One night toward the end of the week, I glanced to my left and saw the offering basket being passed along. This was obviously a custom or the traditional manner they embraced.

God really is our source. Therefore, I gave no further thought about the matter. When the meeting ended, a check for $550.00 was handed to me, the exact amount of money we owed on our taxes. That last night someone also put a hundred dollar bill in my pocket. This more than adequately took care of our expenses for the trip.

We really do serve an awesome God. Someone has said that He is the best Daddy in the whole, wide world. I urge the reader to walk in obedience and, thusly, validate this assertion for him or herself.

Football-Size Tumor Vanishes

Russell was declared terminally ill by his surgeon to be. He had cancer in the worst-way possible. Preoperative tests indicated the presence of a cancerous abdominal tumor.

The follow-up surgery revealed that a medical nightmare existed. A tumor the size of a football inhabited his abdominal cavity. The tentacles of this monster were pervasive beyond removal.

In effect, nothing medically could be done for Rusty. The incision was closed as premature death aggressively encroached upon Rusty. The attending physicians were as gracious as possible in this profoundly difficult time.

I had only met Rusty a couple of times before he became sick. There had never been the opportunity to develop a friendship with him before this tragic diagnosis. However, several of his friends suggested that I go and pray with him.

I am always pleased to respond affirmatively to such urgings. The kindly sick man received me graciously. God, in extreme grace and mercy, released a magnificent miracle in Rusty that very hour.

Later he related to me the details of the beautiful move of God in his body that fateful day:

> "The tumor began to move when you started to pray. You prayed and left my hospital room, but the thing continued movement for about twenty minutes. Then I realized that it was totally gone. It had completely shrunk."

Rusty was later declared cancer free. He consistently shared this testimony with many of his friends. Such conversations are an obedience to the admonition of Jesus Christ as recorded in Mark 5:19 (KJV Bible). In this passage of scripture, Jesus said to one who had received a miracle: "Go home to thy friends and tell them how great things the Lord hath done for thee and hath had compassion on thee."

No Problem Too Big For God

Linda's heart doctor had given her a rather dire prognosis. A CAT scan clearly indicated that her main aorta had deteriorated to a dangerous degree. To reveal accurately the full extent of the problem, a heart catherization was scheduled.

The lady's surgeon had strongly hinted that he expected the test results to mandate open chest surgery. He was anticipating the necessity of an aortic replacement.

While Linda's heart cath was in progress, her family talked seriously about selecting the medical facility where the radical surgery would be conducted. Her doctor had convinced them that the heart cath would reveal the extensive degree of her cardio problems—making cardiovascular surgery necessary.

Before the cath began, I entered the cubicle and prayed for Linda. I asked God for a miracle that would make such a procedure unnecessary.

When the good doctor finished the procedure, he brought a surprise to the family. I heard him say, "No further surgery is necessary. The aorta is not nearly as damaged as we had concluded. We will just keep a watch on the situation. I want to check her again in six months."

Linda's condition remains good. Her conviction is that God divinely reversed her condition as I prayed with her that day. Linda is a Christian of great faith. She, herself, is a divine catalyst for an ongoing, great release of God's power.

Man Healed by Unintentional Touch

This is the most unusual healing of which I have ever been associated. Actually, I have never heard of this happening before. Sandy had a large and painful growth on the back of his neck. I was not aware of this fact when I agreed to help in the situation.

I received a call from my friend Phillip one morning at about 7:00 a.m. Phillip related to me that our mutual friend, Sandy, was headed to his house. "Would you come and help me deal with whatever the issue is?" Phillip requested.

We both listened intently as our visitor sobbed-out his story. His wife was with her family in Georgia because of his errant behavior. He was asking our help in receiving forgiveness for his transgressions. Sandy did not mention any physical problems.

Both Phillip and I shared our hearts with Sandy. Afterwards, I knelt in front of the repentant man who sat on a small couch. He was weeping softly as I began to pray. In the process, I put my right hand on his right shoulder. My left hand was on his left shoulder near his neck.

Rethinking the situation later, I realized that I had gently patted Sandy on his neck while I was praying. Sandy prayed, asking for cleansing and forgiveness. Our friend's face and attitude indicated that absolute peace dawned upon him. Afterwards, I hurried away to other responsibilities.

Later, I would learn about the thrilling miracle that Sandy had received. Immediately after I left, Sandy declared, "My pain is gone, and the knot on my neck has disappeared. Pastor Jack was hitting that growth on my neck while he was praying, and now it's gone."

I had been completely unaware that I was even touching his neck. In retrospect, I realized that I have a habit of gently patting folks on the shoulder while praying for them. Apparently, the growth was so sore that the slightest touch was almost unbearable.

In the Bible's book of Mark, Chapter 15, verses 17-18, we find the remarkable answer to why God healed Sandy. The Scripture admonishes: "These signs shall follow them that believe; they shall lay hands on the sick and they shall recover."

Runaway Boy Brought Home by Prayer

Being a teenager has never been easy. It is more difficult now than at any point in the past. Peer pressure is an unrelenting source of anxiety and despair.

School life in this society is almost a Pandora's Box in our youths' daily lives. Temptations regarding illegal drugs, sexual promiscuity and pressure to excel academically are some of the items in this box.

Items constantly "get out of the box," making life for our youth almost intolerable. The adolescent age group also struggles with acne, inferiority, and rejection. This potentially destructive mentality spawns dangerous moods.

The teen suicide rate is escalating in our fast-paced American society. Teens often contemplate the idea of running away in order to escape to somewhere better. Many of those desperate adolescents who run away are never seen again.

The father of a runaway youth appeared at our church several years ago. Distraught and grieved, Wesley was combing the city asking if anyone had seen his son. By divine providence, this harried dad stopped to inquire of me.

I listened intently as Wes gave a detailed description of his son. I had not seen the fleeing boy.

As the dejected father turned to leave I said, "May I pray with you about this situation?"

His response was, "Yes, yes, please pray for my boy."

I petitioned Father God, in Jesus Name by the power of the Holy Spirit, to send Wesley's son home. I would learn later that within the hour someone delivered the youth home safe and sound. Wes has shared with me, more than once, that he is sure that God heard and answered my prayer.

Betty is Set Free from Fear

The term *fear not* is in the Bible more than three hundred times. This is quite an amazing fact. It clearly indicates that God recognizes that fear is a serious hindrance to His people. The abundant life and fear cannot coexist.

When fear becomes entrenched in the life of a Christian, a serious bondage can result. Fear can enter one's life from sources that are almost without number. It must be recognized that regardless of fear's point of entry, it is always subject to the power of God.

About twenty years ago, our friend Betty was temporarily traumatized and almost immobilized by fear. She was a devout Christian and faithful worshipper in our church. She had wonderfully experienced the supernatural power of God on several occasions. Betty had been miraculously healed more than once in her life.

"The enemy comes to steal and destroy," said Jesus Christ in John 10:10. A dark spirit attempted to do both on Betty's wedding day. Although Fear was unsuccessful in this agenda, it did cause much unrest in the heart of this bride.

Betty recently shared with me her victorious story about overcoming this harassing monster. She reminded me that every day for a week she came for prayer about this matter. The problem did not leave, nor was it diminished by my efforts during these visits.

It became evident that the problem was even more serious than we had perceived: A dark spirit was oppressing Betty. Serious as it was, God was faithful in freeing her from this debilitating bondage.

"The last time that I came to you about the problem," she stated emphatically, "God gave me a miracle. I remember distinctly how this came about," Betty continued. "You gently put your left hand on my chin and said, 'Look me in the eyes. Fear, you come out in the name of Jesus Christ,' you commanded. From that very moment until this one I have been absolutely free from fear," Betty enthusiastically emphasized. Through these many years, she and her husband, Doug, faithfully and obediently serve our Lord.

Pastor's Arthritic Hand Healed

The question, "How are you doing?" is normally just a rhetorical expression. Most of the time, the welfare of the one to whom the question is addressed is not really of any concern.

Too often, the question is merely a polite greeting made in passing to both friends and strangers alike. Usually there is insufficient time to be genuine in such situations.

Truthfully, such questions, when sincerely posed, will often become a divine entrée for a work of God. The true disciple of Jesus Christ can alertly use this question, as well as the response, as a ministry opportunity.

Roy said, "Brother Jack, before you prayed for me, I had not been able to make a fist with my left hand for six months." He then demonstrated his ability to close his fist by waving it around enthusiastically.

Several months before, I had encountered him in the lobby of Riley Memorial Hospital. "I am not doing well," was his response to my question that afternoon. He proceeded to tell me about his painful arthritic hand.

Roy is a local pastor and a true man of God. "May I pray for your hand, my brother?" I asked him sympathetically. Permission granted, I put my right hand on the problem and asked God to release healing into the hand.

As we now stood in Rush Foundation Hospital's lobby, he testified that God, indeed, heard that prayer. Roy thanked me and proceeded to ask me to pray for his other hand.

The moral of this story is that we can effectively minister wherever and whenever we will take the time to ask this question with genuineness. Almost everyone is going through something that merits the prayer of faith from our heart.

The next time you go to your favorite store, take the time to "set people up" with the question, "How are you?" It likely will be an opportunity to pray in the power of the Holy Spirit for a myriad of needs. God is faithful, and you will often see God answer miraculously.

A Big Miracle in a Big Toe

Could something as small as a big toe experience a big miracle? The answer is absolutely, yes! This intriguing story is about a big man and a big toe that was "big-time" infected.

Such a situation results in excruciating pain. Granted, this account is not about something big like cancer, blood poisoning, or heart disease; however, a bad toe condition of this magnitude is definitely a big problem.

This miracle took place in Antioch Baptist Church in House, Mississippi. My friend Daniel was the pastor at that time. We were involved in a pastors' prayer meeting that day.

At these prayer times, all sorts of needs are brought before God. An array of situations was shared on the occasion mentioned above. All pastors present normally interceded for these prayer requests.

After the corporate prayer time had ended, James had a specific request for me. He said, "One of my big toes has a very big problem."

The toe in question was throbbing with pain. My friend said there was discoloration and swelling. "It is," he said, "seriously infected."

I put my hands on Jim's shoulders and asked God to heal that painful toe. God did so immediately. Now this may appear like a small thing, but not so to the person involved. Indeed, the miracle was bigger than Daniel's infected toe. Anyone, who has ever had a badly infected toe, will understand what a big thing God did for Jim.

God's Mercy Prevents Suicide

Suicide is one of life's enormous tragedies. Those left behind have emotional trauma that can be healed only by an out-flowing of God's magnificent love. To God's credit alone, He used me to stop a planned suicide.

The wife, mother and lady of the house, was pushed to the very brink of self-destruction by utter domestic chaos. Before the situation unfolded, I had never met any of this family.

Rose (the name has been changed to protect the innocent) and her family lived in a village about forty miles from where I reside. Out of the blue, this lady called our church office asking for an appointment with me. I had no concept of how very critical the situation was with this person.

In retrospect, this call was the beginning of a very real divine appointment. Rose was a Christian. Her husband, however, had no interest in the things of God. It is no wonder that the teenaged son was the focal point of a great deal of the chaos.

I am a good listener. Rose was in dire need of a nonjudgmental ear. It is my experience that if we ask God to be in charge of such interviews, He absolutely will take charge. He will give revelation to the one who is sharing his or her heart.

The Spirit of God touched Rose anew that very day. The refreshing presence of the Holy Spirit gave hope for every facet of her entangled problem.

Later, I would discover that Rose had carefully planned the mechanics of ending her life that fateful day. Her activities also included the crafting of a suicide note for her family.

After carefully wording her last note, the Holy Spirit mightily moved in her heart. Someone, to whom she had vocalized her pain, suggested that I might be a helpful person with whom to converse.

Thusly began a precious work of the Holy Spirit in Rose. After her encounter with sweet Jesus, she returned home and destroyed the note.

May God give listening ears to each of us! May He grant divine appointments for each of us every day. May He continually equip and empower us by His Spirit to effectively represent Him.

A Diamond Reappears

God delights in bringing back things that seem to have hopelessly disappeared. Often when we give up in our search, the item suddenly reappears. Almost every person to whom prayer is important has had one or more of these magnificent experiences.

The diamond in my wife's wedding ring was the focus of one such thrilling episode in our lives. Most of us men have little concept of the sentimental worth of a lady's wedding ring. Perhaps Father God is the only one who can fathom the depth of a bride's dismay in the face of such a loss.

Around twenty-five years ago, my wife Joy was shaken by the possibility that her diamond was gone forever. We were on a ministry trip to Clinton, Mississippi, when she became aware that her stone was not in its setting.

She had just emerged from the ladies' room at a rest stop on the interstate when the event unfolded. First, we searched the interior of our car thoroughly.

We then retraced her steps to the door of the rest room a couple of times. We realized that the stone could have bounced some distance if it had fallen out as Joy walked briskly toward the facility. Joy meticulously searched the interior of the ladies' room several times in vain.

There were no other females in the toilet at the time, so Joy guarded the door for me to give the room a once over. Before driving away, we went over every possible area, as the saying is, with a fine toothed comb.

The situation appeared hopeless as we continued our trek westward. We had prayed from the beginning of the scenario, and we naturally continued to do so all the way to Clinton.

It was clear that only God could bring forth the diamond. This we requested and thanked Him for it by faith. Upon our arrival at the Clinton residence, I decided to make another hasty check of the auto's interior.

It was one of those rare times when our car was very clean on the inside. In other words, the gem could not possibly be concealed under litter. Once again, I opened the back door of the passenger's side and peered downward.

Right in the center of the floor mat lay the coveted, priceless wedding diamond. It lay there as conspicuous as an egg would have been. Clearly, it had not been there when we drove away from the rest stop.

We had looked under the seat, in the seat and everywhere else in our vehicle. It was as though the object had vanished from the planet.

There is no doubt in my mind that God heard the cry of His daughter. In the process, He brought honor and praise to Himself. The Holy Spirit tells us through the Apostle Paul that God is faithful. For this truth I give Him thanks. For His precious display of grace to my wife, I adore Him.

Stomach Growth Disappears Overnight

Judy Smith Truelove had one of those experiences where God just showed up and showed out. The former statement may not be the best grammar, but it very accurately describes what God did for this lady. This occurrence was actually a defining point in her walk with God.

I have known this lady all of her adult life. Mike Smith was her husband before his early home going to Heaven. He was gentle and kind to family and friends alike. After many years of being alone, Judy met and married Bob Truelove, also an incredibly nice person. He, too, is a follower of Jesus Christ.

Numerous abdominal x-rays clearly exposed the presence of a growth of some nature. It was also obvious that whatever was there was increasing in size. Numerous medications had not succeeded in dealing with this problem.

Judy was twenty-three years old when this problem reached a crisis point. She had been living with a great deal of pain and discomfort for some time.

She was hospitalized and scheduled for a gastrointestinal scope the following morning. The night before the procedure, God entered Judy's room and gave her a physical miracle and a new relationship with Himself.

Mrs. Truelove recently recounted the entire episode with me. That fateful night she was feeling isolated and near panic with fear. She called her mother-in-law, Annie Smith, for comfort and prayer.

Annie, a very godly lady, prayed for Judy and lavished consoling words on her. Realizing that she was not getting through the wall of fear, Annie volunteered to call me, her pastor, and request my prayer support.

I recognized that something more was required than prayer at a distance. I related to Mrs. Smith that I would go immediately to the hospital and pray with her daughter-in-law.

It was past 9:30 p.m. when I received the "emergency" call. It was approximately 10:00p.m. when I arrived at the patient's room .

Judy was surprised that I had come. Not only was it late to make a hospital visit, but it also was a very stormy night. The blustery wind and pelting rain would have been intimidating, except that I had a mandate from my Lord.

During the next thirty minutes or so, this special patient received the peace of God. The storm outside had been symbolic of her storm within.

The good news is that Jesus is still quieting storms in our day. This, however, was the lesser of the good things that God did that night. The presence of the Prince of Peace gave Judy a good night's rest. The best news came the next morning.

The dawn of a new day was to be a new beginning for Judy spiritually and physically. When Judy Smith became fully awake after her procedure, her doctor entered the room. He just stood there for what seemed like an eternity before speaking.

With a huge smile and with hands somewhat lifted up, he said, "I can't understand it. I just do not understand what has happened. The growth is absolutely gone."

Judy, without hesitation, declared, "I understand what happened. God has given me a miracle."

Judy Smith Truelove is still in awe about how God came one dark and stormy night and permanently left a ray of sunshine in her soul. Ask Judy about that night, but make sure you have a little time. Her enthusiasm remains unabated even after all these years.

Truck Brain Healed

The title to this story might seem ridiculous to some folks; however, I ask the reader to consider the evidence before making such an assertion. The vehicle in question is an older Dodge Dakota.

The truck is actually fifteen years old. The transmission is a floor shift with five forward gears. The fifth gear is like an over-drive. Despite its age, the vehicle is really in good condition. It even uses very little oil.

After owning this white-colored jewel for about six months, a problem suddenly surfaced. It seemed to me to be serious because the motor was involved.

The problem would manifest several times on every occasion that I would drive the truck. I would just drive along and suddenly the motor would begin to "rev-up" very loudly. It sounded as though something would surely disintegrate at this excessive burst of rpms.

I inquired of a mechanic friend about what it would take to fix this problem. He related to me that the problem could not be corrected. He explained that it was a malfunction in the truck's brain. Therefore, he stressed that it would be necessary to live with the situation.

The next time that I drove the vehicle, the problem returned. I thought, "Man may not be able to fix the situation, but God can." I immediately began to ask God, in Jesus Name, to fix my truck's brain.

Since that day, about four months ago, the problem has not evidenced again. My conclusion in the matter is obvious and simple. God heard the prayer of His servant and healed the truck's brain.

Amazing Grace in a Graveyard

One of the most notable miracles that Jesus ever did took place in a cemetery. Wherever Jesus went, the power of God was incredibly released to meet needs. Very few people have been privileged to witness a mighty act of God in a place designated to bury the dead. This is just such a story.

Anita was the divine catalyst that initiated the events that led to this God happening. Nita is one of those very godly people who are unusually quiet. She is a strong witness; whenever she does speak, it is important.

Her dad had just been deposited into the earth when she began a conversation that ended in a miracle for one of her relatives. This event took place in the Antioch Baptist Church Cemetery in House, Mississippi. I had the privilege of conducting the funeral.

After the committal service was finished, Anita introduced me to a niece whose name was Bobbie. Somehow, I had not met this relative of Anita's until after we walked away from the grave. In this conversation, I would learn that Bobbie had a very unusual physical problem.

She had a large growth under her right rib cage. When she would bend to the right, the growth would protrude outward. Incredible as it seems, there was no pain involved.

A series of X-rays validated that this abnormal growth was increasing in size. Nita suggested to Bobbie that I be allowed to pray about the problem. Permission granted, I reached out and touched her right arm and asked God to heal my new acquaintance.

A day or two later, Bobbie kept a scheduled appointment to have the situation checked again by the family doctor. It was only a short time before the doctor reentered the exam room and informed Bobbie that the growth had totally disappeared.

Only then, did Anita's niece realize that she had met the Master in a unique way near her uncle's grave. This was truly amazing grace displayed in a graveyard. Be encouraged to reach out to God for a miracle right now.

Sally Testifies of God's Beautiful Intervention: A Witness to God's Power

Because the Father gives to His beloved in sweet sleep, it makes perfect sense that the enemy of our souls would try to rob us of this precious, necessary gift. Despite the fact that I have never enjoyed horror movies or scary books, I have experienced some really horrific dreams and manifestations of evil in my home ….especially during the night.

I have seen disturbing images that some people would describe as mocking spirits, move through my house to taunt me in the night. I have heard strange noises from inanimate objects in my room. Moreover, I was taught to pray and confront those issues with the Word of God. I knew in my intellect that simple prayers could alleviate such torment. However, I was one of those people who endured hardship because of my hesitation to apply God's Word. I am so grateful to have learned the truth.

During a period when I felt particularly weak and vulnerable, the unexplained noises and strange experiences began to intensify in my home. One morning, I woke to find the lamp from my bedside table in the middle of the floor. I called for help. Four of the most Godly prayer warriors that I know, including Jack and Joy Giles, graciously agreed to come to my home to pray.

They walked through my home and helped identify objects that might be harmful or not edifying. With their support and encouragement, I was able to let go of some objects that held some financial or sentimental value but were identified as being spiritually detrimental in my home.

The sky did not visibly split open over my home. I did not experience any physical sensations indicating change. I did not feel any differently, but the days following the visit of Christians committed to sincere prayer, the disturbances stopped, and I was able to sleep more peacefully. Wise counsel, just like sleep, is truly one of God's greatest gifts; for me, it is miraculous. It is humbling to see God's gifts manifested in such a simple, powerful way.

God Answers an Unusual Prayer for Children

How much does God pay attention to the whims of little boys and girls? Is God perhaps too busy to notice the sudden thoughts and expressions uttered by excited children? An experience by two of our grandchildren speaks clearly to this question.

My wife, Joy, and I shared this treasured event. We were traveling with our son, Mike, his wife, Kathy, and their three children. We were regaling ancient churches, pioneer cabins, and an array of wildlife and other phenomenon when surprised by this adventure.

This occurrence took place in one of nature's most magnificent places. We were in Cades Cove, which is a part of the Great Smoky Mountains National Parks. Beautiful sights abound everywhere one looks.

We were about halfway around Cades Cove when Mikayla, a preteen), and Jackie, a teenager, said almost simultaneously, "We would like to see a bear." This was the first week in December.

Their Dad responded matter-of-factly, "The bears are already in hibernation this time of the year."

My response was a bold audible prayer, "Lord, please let these girls see a bear."

It was really quiet in the van for a few minutes when someone cried out, "Look, there is a bear!"

Sure enough, there was a huge black bear about 150 feet from the road. This majestic animal was in a large field eating acorns and totally oblivious to the excited humans nearby.

It is my persuasion that God orchestrated this encounter just for the children. The Bible is clear that God loves children. My grandchildren sensed that God had heard their heart's cry. This is also a strong conviction of my heart.

Two Alcoholics set free at the Same Time

A very well known cliché is, "Once an alcoholic, always an alcoholic." Those who embrace this philosophy aid in creating an atmosphere of hopelessness and desperation for victims of this horrific bondage. Christians who espouse this position need seriously to rethink this issue.

This conclusion espouses a doctrine called humanism and is not Biblical Christianity. No right-thinking person would deny that alcoholism is a blight on the human race. All of us understand that the Bible declares that nothing is impossible with God. It is high time that we embrace this truth at face value.

This truth certainly includes the possibility of setting folks free of addictions. The number of precious souls delivered each year in this nation is countless. The majority of these victories is a direct result of Christ centered rehabilitation centers. There are occasions, however, when individuals find freedom through personal ministry.

This is an eyewitness account of a husband and wife who God delivered from addiction at the same time. This is a beautiful example of another method that God sometimes uses in destroying bondages. Their names were Al and Mary. They had been married for several years when this magnificent experience took place. Long before they married, both of them had been held captive by this evil monster.

This dear lady was a distant relative of mine. She was kind, gentle and very quiet. Her disposition was marked by excessive gloom and sadness. Al's emotional make-up was very much like that of his wife.

My relationship with the two had always been pleasant but very casual. They had erected a wall around themselves, and no one was allowed past that wall. Mary had always called me by my middle name, which is O'Neil.

I received a surprise telephone call from Mary one morning. I had not seen or heard from them for a couple of years. "Neil, honey," she pleaded, "would you come and pray for Al and me as soon as possible?"

"Yes, certainly," I replied, "Please give me your address."

My visit with this precious couple was a divine appointment. They were both humble and contrite, freely admitting that they were powerless to help themselves.

In my fifty years of ministry, I have never seen a greater work than God did that day. There was no flash of lightning, peal of thunder, or other overt drama; but they were never the same after that occasion.

The miracle that transpired that day was solely due to the power of the Holy Spirit. My heartfelt cry to God for them was that He might manifest mercy and set them free. Neither of them took another drink of booze the rest of their lives.

God is awesome beyond description. A thousand years would be insufficient time to praise Him for the display of amazing grace in making this couple free from the dregs of alcoholism.

Troubled Medical Doctor Receives Miracle

Paul was a medical doctor with many good qualities. He was well liked by his patients and peers alike. He was kind, compassionate and religious. He was seriously concerned about his patients' well-being.

Paul, however, had a very serious problem. He was an alcoholic. When I met him, he had recently been barred from the third hospital because of this problem. In addition, he had lost two families in this downward moral spiral.

One of his aunts was a dear friend to my wife, Joy, and me. Her name was Edith. God had used Joy and me to bring a miracle into the life of this lady's daughter, Mary.

When Edith became aware of this great work of God in her daughter, she approached me about her nephew. "I would like you to pray for my nephew Paul," she declared. She continued by sharing the particulars of his extensive drinking problem.

She almost considered Paul to be in a situation beyond hope. He had run away from the last treatment center in which he had sought help.

"Currently," she confided, "we have no idea where he might be located. Would you minister to him if I can manage to get him to my home?" she asked. I realized that I could not help Paul, but I knew well that God could set him free.

Within a week, Edith called to say, "Paul is here. Please come as soon as possible."

I interviewed Paul and discovered that he, indeed, was a believer in Jesus Christ. He was a member of a branch of the Presbyterian Church.

The bottom line was that Paul really wanted to be free of his addiction to alcohol. He was sick and tired of the direction in which his life was going. He wanted to hear what I had to say.

I shared extensively with Paul about spiritual warfare. He received all that I shared as a Word from God to him. He acknowledged his sin and asked God to forgive him.

Miraculously, Paul was set free from this bondage of addiction that wonderful day. For several years now, Edith's nephew has been the director of a well known-rehabilitation hospital in the State of Mississippi. He is another precious soul who has experienced a divine epiphany.

Former Green Bay Packer Receives Miracle

The ability to play professional football is an extraordinary achievement. Both great talent and unusual strength are essential in this quest. Being in the right place at the right time is also critically important.

Many very good players are never selected because of a lack of publicity or some other extenuating circumstance. My friend, Steve, graduated from the University of Southern Mississippi where he excelled as a punter. He was, however, overlooked in the National Football League Draft.

Incredibly, a year or two later, Steve was signed by the Green Bay Packers. It was as though fate smiled on him. The Packers were holding tryouts at Gulfport High School when this happened.

Of the two hundred trying out, he was the only one selected. This intriguing story is like a fairy tale, like something out of a movie. This magnificent moment, however, was all too brief.

A very promising career by an outstanding athlete was cut short by a devastating injury. As disappointing as this was, it was the least of two life-altering happenings. The more serious one was that Steve became an alcoholic.

This individual possesses many good characteristics. He is also loved by many godly people. Nevertheless, his bondage became a horrific blight on his life.

The personal cost to Steve and his family was devastating and heartbreaking. Before the "Hound of Heaven" finally apprehended Steve, the alcoholism had continued for more than twenty-five years.

About four years ago that vicious cycle in his life was finally broken. By the magnificent grace of God, he was granted a new beginning. He was near graduation from a Christian rehabilitation facility at that time.

The beginning of Steve's divine epiphany was when I received a call from the director of the rehab. He requested that I come to their place of ministry as soon as possible. "We need your help with two men," the director stated. “They are really good men,” he continued, “but we can’t seem to help them. These guys are more than just clients, they are personal friends. We love them and need your assistance in reaching them,” he reiterated.

Upon my arrival, the director shared with me these men’s tragic stories. Furthermore, I was asked to preach in the chapel service that night.

It was also requested of me not to tell Steve that I was there specifically to minister to him and the other gentleman. I thought, “Lord, how am I going to be able to pull this off?”

After preaching that night, I was again in awe of God’s scheduling ability. Upon finishing the message, the very first person to approach me said, “My name is Steve, and I really need to talk to you sometime soon.”

I am still amazed when God orchestrates these divine appointments. Somehow, in the providence of God the Almighty, this was Steve’s time. Had he not responded affirmatively, there may not have been another opportunity.

I made a permanent friend that day. God made my new friend a transformed man during our time with the Savior that afternoon. A couple of months later, Steve graduated and was asked to remain on campus and work with the ministry in the area of alumni relations.

A few days ago, the executive director of the facility shared with me that Steve remains a true trophy of God’s grace. Steve also continues to work to build stronger relationships between graduates and that ministry. It should be noted that he is among a group of strong prayer warriors who are available to intercede for any request that comes their way.

Evelyn's Eye Miracle

For the past fifteen years I have had a problem called "low tension glaucoma" in both of my eyes! This condition has required frequent trips to a specialist in Jackson, Mississippi.

Last week my local eye doctor said, "You have to go back to Jackson. Your pressure is higher than it has ever been. Your optic nerves have to be checked. I'm going to add another drop to try and get the pressure down. After you go to Jackson, Dr. Herrington will tell me what to do."

I left my doctor's office thinking, "I hate going to Jackson." I cried all the way home last time. My doctor told me that I was going blind. He said there was no way to correct the damage already done.

My appointment in Jackson was October 10, 2010. I made plans for someone to take me to Herrington's clinic. I also prayed for a safe trip.

After my arrival, several tests were conducted before the doctor arrived. He sat at his desk with his back to me as he looked over the report of the tests that had just been completed.

Then he said over and over, "I don't believe this. This has never been done, it's a miracle."

After he said the word *miracle* three times, I said, "Well, are you going to tell me?"

He then turned around, looking at me and said, "It's been ten years since I last saw you, and the optic nerves are the same. I have never seen that happen before."

I said, "Well, some people don't believe in God. Do you?"

He said, "I do."

I said to him, "Ten years ago, I told God that I knew that damage had been done; I asked Him to stabilize my eyes and not allow them to get any worse. For all these years, this has been my prayer, and you have just confirmed that God has heard my heart cry."

The doctor then pulled his chair up close, pointed his finger at me and said, "If that's what you did, keep doing it. It is working; I will let your doctor know what drops to add. It has been a pleasure seeing you today."

This time I came home from Jackson with a song in my heart. It was, as you might have guessed, "Jesus Loves Me."

God and our Small Problems or Concerns

There are some who erroneously think that God should not be bothered with our small problems. Whether a problem is small or large actually has to do with one's personal perspective rather than a genuine Biblical truth that can be validated scripturally.

Consider with me Jennifer's problem. This lady had done something rather special for our church. I placed a call to her in order to express my appreciation for this act of kindness but instead left a message on her voice mail.

When she returned my call a few hours later, I could hardly understand what she was saying. With a great deal of difficulty, she was able to communicate that she was struggling with extreme laryngitis.

I expressed my sympathy and related my thanks for her caring spirit of generosity. Before ending the call, I offered to pray for this friend of God.

In my prayer, I rebuked the root cause of her throat condition. I prayed in the name of Jesus Christ. About five minutes later, Jennifer called back rejoicing and fully healed.

The Holy Spirit says to us in one of Peter's letters that we are invited to cast all of our cares on Him (the Lord Jesus) because He cares for us (I Peter 5:7). He said nothing about the size of the problems; we are to bring them all to our precious and wonderful Father God.

Pastor Healed of Nagging Back Problem

Tommy is an extraordinarily gifted man of God. The impartations of grace by the Holy Spirit include preaching, prophecy, singing and song writing. I also have a strong suspicion that there are other areas of anointing entrusted to this man.

When I first met Tommy, he was pastoring a Southern Baptist Church in Kemper County, near Daleville, Mississippi. I became acquainted with him because I had relatives that attended the fellowship of which he was the head Elder. At the time this story unfolded, we were merely acquainted.

With no prior notice, he just showed up at my church office one day. I never learned the specific purpose for which he came. Scripture and the things of God were the focus of our conversation during our sharing time. As Tommy prepared to leave, he suddenly said, "Bro. Jack, I am constantly bothered by an aggravating back pain. Will you please pray for me?"

It is always very satisfying when someone requests that I pray for them. I, in a very simple and straightforward way, asked God to heal my fellow pastor. I did not see Tommy nor even think about this experience for several years.

About seven years later, I was invited to minister in his church in North Mississippi. It was during this visit that he related to me that God had healed his back that day in the office of Macedonia Baptist Church.

Pastor Healed Emotionally in Worship Time

There is much healing that needs to take place in the family of God. Immediately one visualizes several kinds of hurt that absolutely requires divine intervention to produce wellness, wholeness or healing. The magnificent truth is that all these healings can still take place. However, heart sickness is the most overlooked of all human pain.

When a person's heart is broken, his or her whole being is disturbed, distraught and sick, which causes the process of complete deterioration to begin. God's answer for his crises is found in the Bible's book of Luke, Chapter 4, verses 18- 19. These two verses comprise the message and mission of Jesus Christ, Messiah and King.

The primary mission of our Messiah was to reconcile men unto Himself. In II Corinthians 5:17-19, the Holy Spirit clearly restates this truth to us through the Apostle Paul.

The last sentence in verse 18 in Luke Chapter Four is incredible and precious. The New American Standard Bible reads that Jesus purposes to "set free those who are downtrodden." Inherent in this phrase is that Christ came to heal hearts that are "broken in pieces."

There are literally multitudes in churches across our communities whose hearts have been broken from a vast array of causes. Again, let it be clearly understood, that Jesus Christ came into this sin scarred war zone to also specifically address this issue. It is likely that every person who reads this story is in need of a heart healing because of some terrible experience in his or her past.

This story is the testimony to how this author received healing for a broken heart. Your situation and story will likely be very different, but the Healer's power, love and grace are also sufficient for you and available to you.

I went through about three months of extreme emotional anguish. A familiar friend had become insubordinate and contentious. The potential for widening discord and subsequent disaster became evident.

During this time, I ate little and slept fitfully. I did, however, pray without ceasing. My heart-pain brought me to the brink of resigning as pastor of my current church.

My gracious Lord, however, brought the ungodly matter to a victorious conclusion at the Cornerstone Christian Fellowship in New Orleans, Louisiana. My wife and I were attending a conference in this great church with Pastor Jimmy Autry.

I was on their schedule to preach Saturday morning. At some point on Friday, I made the decision to resign upon my return home. I could no longer bear my pain. I also realized that it would not be possible for me to preach the following morning.

Worship in the service that night was powerful. During this wonderful time that Friday night, I continually cried out to God. My anguished soul pleaded for God to heal my heart.

Suddenly and lavishly, the Holy Spirit invaded and overwhelmed my whole being. My bruised and battered heart was instantaneously sick no more.

Father God had heard and run to His wounded son. This experience was an absolute epiphany. I was, indeed, anointed to preach the next morning.

My conviction of the incredible value of worship was greatly heightened that beautiful night. The Holy Spirit declared through King David, "God inhabits the praises of His people" (Psalms 22:3). When I reflect on my life and ministry-saving experience of that holy night, all I can say is, "Thank you sweet, precious Lord."

Joy Is Healed from Severe Asthma

As a young child, I had frequent bouts with bronchitis. I was improving under the care of our family physician when he was suddenly drafted into service during World War II. After that time, I grew steadily worse and began to suffer asthmatic attacks.

In my teens, the asthma worsened, and I had year-round problems. However, I was much better in the summer. Many times, upon waiting for the medication to take effect, I could only get some relief by the massaging of my back. Mama and Daddy Pat would untiringly rub my back at these times. After I married, Jack took on this responsibility and never seemed to tire or at least complain if he did.

The emergency room of the hospital or a doctor's office was the place where I went for an injection to get relief. I tried to avoid this if I could get relief at home. I just did not feel like getting out of the house during these flare-up episodes.

Trying to stay in school was a difficult task. I did not feel like going anywhere in the mornings, especially if I had been up at night struggling to breathe. I managed to get to my senior year in high school but experienced so much illness that I had to drop two of my courses. Therefore, I attended only half the school day. I missed close to half a year. Nevertheless, I managed to graduate with my class.

Led by the Lord to go to college, I was able to get through one nine-week term before the asthma attacks became so frequent that I had to drop out. I was determined to get back to college, and I did so when the summer term started. There, I met Jack, and I knew why God had led me to go to college.

Jack and I dated and 1 ½ years later we married. We had three young children by the time I was twenty-nine. The asthma had been a part of my life for so long that I just tolerated the illness. It had not entered my mind that my Father in Heaven might heal me if I asked.

I felt hopelessness after being told by my doctor that I needed further help or the asthma might evolve into emphysema. My doctor suggested that I go to an allergy specialist.

Taking my doctor's advice, I became the patient of a specialist for about four years. Still, my health improved very little. After the doctor said he had never treated any one longer than four years, I stopped the medical appointments.

I was standing under my clothesline one day when, in almost despair, I cried out to my heavenly Father to heal me or take me to heaven. It was just too hard physically to continue living as I was.

The miracle happened! I was healed; no longer do I suffer with asthma, a debilitating breathing disease. My miracle happened when I was about thirty-four years old.

Today, at seventy-five years old, I can praise my Father in Heaven who does all things well. Jesus said, "Ask and it shall be given you, seek and you shall find, knock and the door will be opened" (Matthew 7:7).

Grandma Myrtle Saved from Fatal Disease

Myrtle was almost ninety-one years old when she was declared terminally ill. A fatal blood disease befell her. After a considerable stay in the Hinds General Hospital and numerous blood transfusions, she was sent home to die.

The medical care of this lady was then entrusted to a hospice in Jackson, Mississippi. Myrtle was given the prognosis of terminal for her condition, sad beyond belief. Evaluating her condition on a scale of one to ten, with one being the worst, Myrtle was judged a minus one. Her dismal prognosis was shared with the family in order to help them prepare for the inevitable.

Myrtle was my mother-in-law. I am convinced that no one ever had a better mother-in-law than I. She impacted her children and grandchildren in a powerfully positive way. She loved all her family equally and in a very unselfish way.

All the family began to pray often for Grandma Myrtle. For ten consecutive weeks, Myrtle received an upgraded report from the hospice. After eleven full weeks, the health facility concluded that Myrtle no longer needed its services.

At this point, there was no evidence of the blood disease that had threatened her survival. Everyone was astonished and applauded this marvelous medical miracle.

Grandma Myrtle lived for two more years. Her departure from this life had much to do with complications from a broken hip. My opinion is that she would have lived past one hundred had she not experienced a major trauma with the broken hip.

I am also certain that healing power was released to her through the unified praying of the entire family. Concerted prayer was the divine catalyst for her amazing recovery.

It is my observation that Mamaw Myrtle lost her will to live as result of her tragic fall. The intensity of prolonged pain and her subsequent lack of mobility were emotionally devastating to this regal and independent lady.

Approximate to her fall, Myrtle's heavenly mansion was probably just being finished. Her grand and precious Father above then looked upon her with favor and dispatched an angel to deliver her safely to that eternal home. Our entire family was very blessed by this lady who loved all with Godly abandonment.

Chinese Lion Dog Healed

There are two lessons about prayer in this story that need to be pondered, received and emulated by everyone. First, prayer offered in faith will bring about significant intervention from our mighty God. Secondly, there is nothing impossible to God.

Liz and Jerry have owned at least two dogs that have experienced healing by the power of God. Most likely, their deep love for their pets is the foundational reason why God granted these miracles.

This particular little dog is of the Shih Tzu (SHEET-sue) breed. These little beauties are alert, happy, playful and affectionate. In addition, they are hardy creatures who like to be with people.

Gizmo is the name of this outstanding Shih Tzu. The color of this delightful critter is mostly blond with some blotches of white.

Gizmo was a shamefully abused puppy when my friends discovered this rare canine jewel. Time would demonstrate that this adorable pooch would become a large blessing to this couple. This puppy would have died a slow and painful death had the Lord God not brought about his rescue through the Bratus.

I was visiting in their home about a year ago when Jerry asked me to pray for their beloved adopted tyke. For most of his life, Gizmo had endured a heart-wrenching problem. Often he would suffer severe spells of coughing and choking that produced vomiting. I am convinced that God honored the Bratus' intense devotion to a special little creation by an act of sovereign healing. Jerry held Gizmo on his lap while I quietly uttered a prayer of faith. I implored Father God in Jesus name to heal and restore to health this pet that is so important to both Liz and Jerry.

For several years, Jerry was the only human with whom Gizmo spent most of his time. Consequently, they were nearly inseparable during that time frame. If Jerry went to his workshop to tinker on his ole ugly truck, or made a quick trip to Marvin's Building Supply, Gizmo insisted on being there. Even now, this faithful pet takes a nap daily on Jerry's lap.

Now that Liz has retired from her job as a registered nurse, Gizmo's affection has taken a decided bent toward the lady of the house. Actually, the Shih Tzu breed has a way of capturing the devotion of the entire household. Gizmo has certainly been no exception.

The critically important issue in the entire matter is one of love. The couple and this unique canine breed absolutely have a profound mutual admiration for each other. God loves this trio enormously, and I am convinced, smiles when He views their relationship.

The reader would be interested to know that Gizmo's breed is Tibetan or Chinese. The original meaning of the name of this quaint animal Shih Tzu is "lion dog."

Vernon's Leg Saved from Amputation

The doctor very carefully inspected Vernon's left foot and leg. His toes and foot were turning an unsightly purple, and the ugly discoloration seemed to be snaking upward like a deadly viper. The doctor peeled off his latex gloves and without flinching dropped a verbal bomb-shell on the patient.

I observed this entire proceeding from a bird's-eye view. I was in the patient's room and felt the powerful emotional jolt of the physician's declaration. You see, Vernon was my dad.

"Vernon," he declared, "tomorrow, it will be necessary for me to remove your leg just below the knee."

"Absolutely not," dad shot back at the well-known surgeon. The doctor did not take no easily, but obviously, it was Dad's call to make.

The doctor was certain that his decision was right, and Dad was just as adamant that his was the correct choice. Dad's life was in the balance, and all the family recognized this reality.

During the next forty-eight hours, heaven was bombarded on behalf of Vernon Giles' leg. Early in the morning, as the medical personnel peered anxiously at the contested flesh, it was obvious that something incredibly good had taken place. Amputation was no longer a question.

My conviction is that the Holy Spirit had brooded over Dad's dying leg in the doctor's absence. Vernon's miracle was definitely the result of a family united in prayer.

The Problem with Words like Terminal

Words like "terminal" or "irreversible" are absolute emotional blockbusters. Words of such severe negativity often tend to destroy whatever ray of hope that may be left for a sufferer or for his or her loved ones.

Making these pronouncements is the result of human error and/or a lack of knowledge. Such conclusions are reached without the most significant of all factors: The advice of an ever-present God with whom nothing is ever impossible.

Twice in my Dad's eighty-third year, he was the recipient of ominous medical miscalculations. Prayer was the factor that rendered these well-meaning, expert medical conclusions incorrect.

Dad spent five weeks as a patient in the Caraway Methodist Medical Center in Birmingham, Alabama. He was there to utilize their hyperbaric expertise in the healing of wounds. During this specific time, the Birmingham facility was the nearest center offering hyperbaric treatment. In conjunction to this procedure, surgery was done on both of Dad's feet.

The Caraway Medical Center was excellent in every way. Their Chief of Staff would call me every week and provide me with a complete update on Dad's condition. His feet were far from well when other considerations made it necessary for him to return home.

One day after his return home, he passed out and was transferred by ambulance to Riley Memorial Hospital in Meridian, Mississippi. He was diagnosed as having an abdominal blockage that required immediate surgery.

Soon after the procedure was complete, his doctor reported to our family that no blockage was present. He stated to us that Dad's entire digestive system had stopped functioning and would never work again. The physician contributed the cause of this calamity to a lifetime of smoking cigarettes, along with the acute ravages of diabetes over the years.

We received the report of the sympathetic physician courteously.

We viewed this report as a slow death sentence given to our Dad. We shared with this fine physician that we believed that God would restore our Dad.

Dad was in the intensive care unit at Riley's Hospital for several days after the surgery. I had given the nurses in the unit the medicine for Dad's feet that we brought back from the hospital in Birmingham. Shortly after dad entered the unit, one of his nurses approached me and shared that Dad's feet were well and didn't need to be treated any longer.

"What should we do with the medicine that is left over?" She questioned me. My response was that I would call his doctor in Birmingham and ask if we should keep it for some future situation. This medication was a special concoction made in the laboratory at Caraway, and actually had some of Dad's blood in it.

I quickly got in touch with the very kind doctor in Dad's former hospital and shared with him my question. His response was absolutely incredible, "Mr. Giles, you are mistaken. Your father's feet cannot be well. If they actually were well, it would be a superhuman achievement."

"I have the nurse's name that provided me with the information, along with the unit's telephone number, plus permission for you to contact the lady," was my gentle response.

"I will call right now," promised this excellent doctor.

When the Caraway doctor learned the truth from the nurse, he simply told her to dispose of the medicine. This doctor in Birmingham, Alabama, merely provided verification to us that Vernon Giles had indeed received a supernatural healing for his feet.

In addition to this, my Dad's intestinal system did begin to function again in a short time. These two miracles also were the result of corporate prayer. Various family members, along with the churches that they attended, sought God fervently in these matters.

Do not be discouraged by negative words from anyone who speaks despairingly about your sick loved ones. Rather, bring your fervent praying to a new level and involve as many people as possible in your prayer efforts. God is indeed faithful.

Small Boy's Prayer Part of Miracle

Gabe is a delightful three-year-old boy. He is quite an astute child. It can be aptly said of this wee human being that he is "one of the sharpest knives in the drawer." He lives on a rural Newton County, Mississippi, farm along with three others.

Two of those in the home are his doting Mom and Dad. The remaining occupant is Gabe's playmate and bodyguard. This is a creature named Alice. She is a large and very valuable Boxer. Her colors are a strikingly handsome fawn that is offset with white markings.

Alice is a housedog and, therefore, is seldom out of the sight of the little guy who is her master. On a recent Sunday morning, Gabe's community awoke in the clutches of an ice storm. Into this highly dangerous weather condition, Alice disappeared. The family frantically searched for Alice for hours in extreme cold, to no avail.

Gabe's parents are Mickey and Berea. They began a fervent and persistent prayer effort in behalf of their son's beloved dog. Berea's mom, Darnell, also called and solicited my prayer involvement.

Gabe, powerfully moved by his love for Alice, began marathon praying. His prayer was, "Dear God, please bring my Alice home to me, safe and sound. Amen." His mom estimates that she heard him pray this prayer for at least a hundred times.

Berea shared that there were times during this crisis when Gabe was alone in his room and was supposedly watching television, yet she could hear his voice. She would peep into the room, and though the TV set was playing, his back would be to it and he would be asking God to bring Alice back to him.

On Tuesday night the situation became grim because Alice had been out in the horrendous weather for more than thirty hours. At this point, God answered the prayers of His desperate children. Alice was found sitting on the front steps of a church, not far from Gabe's home, at about 8:30 at night.

There are at least three important issues in this beautiful story that should be noted. The first has to do with the special love that God has for children. Gabe's precious heavenly Father facilitated Alice's discovery because of His overflowing heart of love for the child.

The second critically important part of this happy conclusion is the activity of a thing called corporate prayer. When the family of God rallies together in an unceasing prayer effort, for whatever cause, miracles are often birthed.

It is also very interesting that Alice was on the steps of a house of worship when she was found. Most likely, the Spirit of our awesome God was so upon the church that the gentle animal was drawn to wait there for rescue.

"Thank you God for bringing my Alice back to me, safe and sound. Amen," was Gabe's joyful response when given the good news of his pet's return. Thirdly, this diminutive child has learned a lesson in prayer that will not leave him for the rest of his life.

Cervical Cancer Vanquished by Prayer

You will be powerfully stirred and inspired by this amazing story. It will not fail to stretch your soul and enlarge your faith. The normal response to this intriguing act of God is "wow, amazing or beautiful."

Berea is an outstanding Christian lady who is in her late twenties. Her husband is Mickey; and they have a bright, energetic three-year-old boy, that they call Gabe.

Because of the power of corporate prayer, Berea stared death in the face and saw the ugly, evil thing annihilated or blown away. Two doctors in Meridian, Mississippi, agreed that she had multiple problems of a very serious nature. A diagnosis such as Berea received would normally be considered a death sentence.

She had been having stomach problems, but had no idea what the real issues were. Fever, nausea and intense pain had been plaguing Berea for some time. Both a colon scope and a CAT scan were administered, but no doctor or nurse communicated with the lady regarding the test results.

Searching for answers, Berea called one of her local doctors and got the shock of her life. She was informed by the physician's nurse that an appointment had just been made for her in Flowood, Mississippi, with an OB-GYN Doctor.

The time of day, at that moment, was nine in the morning, and she was instructed that it was imperative for her to be in Flowood in two hours. This was about a ninety-mile trip.

Upon arrival at the Flowood hospital, she was given information that was mind-boggling. She was informed that her Meridian CAT scan showed that she had cervical cancer, cysts on her kidneys and ovaries, plus other gynecological abnormalities.

Berea was admitted to the hospital and immediately given an ultrasound and blood work. The surgeon arrived shortly and indicated that their tests verified the presence of a very large malignant mass attached to all her female organs. Immediate surgery was, therefore, a medical mandate.

The patient was then also told that she might wake up with a colostomy bag, a hysterectomy, and with her appendix removed. As soon as the surgeon left the room, Berea says that she "became very scared."

Darnell, Berea's mom, had telephoned me for prayer while they were traveling to the Flowood hospital. I asked God for a miracle during that prayer. Having been told that she would have surgery at 8:00, Berea requested, "Call Bro. Jack and tell him what is happening."

This was on a Wednesday night, and Darnell's call was logged on my cell phone during prayer meeting. I returned her call at about 7:45 and again asked God to remove all disease and sickness from Berea.

Almost everyone had left the church building by this time. I was able, however, to share Berea's dire prognosis with several couples; they began immediately to pray for her complete healing.

Berea's abdomen was opened to the surprised eyes of several physicians. The mass that had been obvious to them just hours before was now gone. Berea, herself, related to me that she too had prayed and felt that the medical people were not going to find anything wrong in her body.

The next morning her OB-GYN nurse in came and shared that "someone" much bigger than the doctors was responsible for her good news, and that she was indeed a miracle. Berea was at home by lunchtime the next day.

This amazing occurrence was the result of corporate prayer. One should never, never underestimate the magnitude of what can happen as a result of the unified prayers of fearless and fervent Christians.

Broken Old Biker Finds Fountain of Youth

George was a man who had lost hope. He had been in jail numerous times. Unfortunately, the Florida State Penitentiary had also been his home for a lengthy period. He once told me that he would never go back to the "Pen" again, that death would be preferable.

He had been betrayed, battered and bruised by the Evil One. George was broken emotionally, physically and financially by a sinful life. He had become an old man way before his time.

Suicide was on his mind when I met him. This was the issue that brought him into my life. Because he dared to cry out to a kind stranger, God brought him to the discovery of a wonderful place where he could begin again.

A special and godly lady named Hazel facilitated our becoming acquainted. Making the world a better place was the agenda that motivated this delightful believer. She might be described as a political activist who was committed to positive change through the church of Jesus Christ. She was a divine catalyst for success in many areas of social concern in her locality. She was quietly persistent in the areas of concern that she sensed God was leading her to address.

Hazel telephoned me one day and said, "Pastor, I need for you to do me a favor."

"And what might that be Hazel?" I responded. She proceeded to share that recently she had experienced car trouble, so it had been necessary to stop in the parking lot of a roadhouse or honky-tonk.

One of the establishment's patrons very kindly helped solve her vehicle problem. In the process, he discovered both a listening ear and a divine appointment. This truly lost soul poured out his hurting heart to an angel of mercy.

Hazel shared with her new friend that there was hope for him through Jesus Christ. She asked George if she might send her pastor to offer additional guidance and direction for his life. His answer was a resounding "yes," but somehow the clergyman never followed through with this opportunity.

It was several weeks later that the urgent call came to me about a man who was struggling with suicidal tendencies. Hazel did not know his full name or where he lived. She just knew that he hung out at this particular bar and that I could locate him with this information.

She was correct in this assumption. I walked right into the tavern and asked where I could find George. The barkeep shot the question to me, “What do you want with George?”

I was given clear and specific directions to where George resided. This happened on a Saturday afternoon. I shared extensively with George and invited him to attend church the next morning. That afternoon the despondent man looked in every way like one who had given up on life.

When I picked him up on Sunday morning, he was clean, neat and all spiffed up. He was well received by our church family and really enjoyed the worship service.

Actually, George was the picture of a thrown away human being. His health was very bad. He had been a heavy drinker and smoker for a very long time. His eating habits were atrocious. His appearance was one of total negligence.

He walked with a decided limp. One leg was broken half way between the knee and ankle. The bone had never mended. I never knew whether this was the result of a fight or an accident.

The day after his first church attendance with us, I returned to George’s home for another visit. My new friend admitted that he was sick and tired of being sick and tired. He acknowledged that he was truly lost and that he could do nothing to better his situation.

I shared with him that Jesus Christ, on the Cross, had assumed the legal responsibility for all our sins. George came to understand that when he chose to receive Jesus Christ into his heart, he would then and there be reborn spiritually.

The Holy Spirit said through Zechariah that there would come a day when a fountain would be opened for sin and impurity (Zachariah 13:1). This prophet of old was referring to a spiritual phenomenon which would allow all mankind the option to begin life over again.

George made this choice that day, and his life was wonderfully and permanently transformed. He asked for Christian baptism the very next Sunday. For two years this new creation in Christ was faithful to worship with us on a regular basis.

Soon after becoming a Christian, George began to dream about a new beginning vocationally. He had always wanted to become a motorcycle mechanic, he passionately shared with us. We prayed often with him about this dream that God had resurrected in his heart.

Our Lord worked out the details for George to move back to Florida and to begin his training as a motorcycle repairman. For a long time we corresponded with our budding bike grease monkey. He continued to follow the Lord and found happiness in the fulfillment of his heart quest.

A Surprising and Beautiful Miracle

The magnificence of God is often displayed through His ingenuity and creativity. These unique qualities are frequently evidenced in ways that amaze all those who love Him. My precious Lord recently surprised me beautifully in such manifestations.

My doctor said, "Pastor, you have a cancer on your face; it needs to be removed as soon as possible." This was a surprise to me. I had gone to my family physician because I was suffering from a hacking cough and needed relief before time to preach on Sunday.

The place on my cheek was about the size of the end of my little finger and was obviously an abnormality. The doctor's office proceeded to set me up with a specialist for surgery. I, along with others, prayed that God would miraculously remove the questionable area on my face.

Surgery day rolled around, and my unwanted facial blemish was still a prominent part of my anatomy. I was to experience a couple of negative surprises during that procedure. First, the surgeon said, "Pastor, never let another one of these get this big before taking care of it."

The second surprise had to do with how many times my face was injected with pain killer for the surgery. The attending doctor drew a circle around the problem area with a marker of some kind. He then proceeded to inject my epidermis six or eight times with a deadening drug.

The entire procedure went flawlessly and concluded in about twenty minutes. The attending nurse then cleaned up my face and bandaged the incision. She instructed me to leave the bandage on overnight because of temporary drainage. I left the office armed with a prescription for pain when my face awakened from the surgery sedation.

The next day was filled with amazement for me. First, I was amazed at the size of the incision on my right cheek. I scrounged up a tape measure and measured the length of the surgeon's cut on my face. It was one and one half inches running up and down.

In addition to the scalpel's opening, the growth was then extricated.

The closure of the flesh had been accomplished by six or seven stitches. This surgical correction had been finished at about 11:30 a.m.

On the way home, I dropped off the prescription for pain medication at the local Wal-Mart Pharmacy. Our son, Mark, retrieved it for me later in the day.

Now, I will share a beautiful and magnificent miracle that took place in my life during the correction of this problem. At no point after the surgery was there any pain. Actually, there had been absolutely no discomfort at all. The pain prescription was never needed.

Considering the size of the incision, removal of a growth and the numerous sutures used, logic shouts that some degree of pain was inevitable. God has again intervened significantly in my life. I cherish this miracle and will praise my Christ for it all the days of my life.

Sickness Caused by a Spirit

"My doctor says that I have crippling arthritis," the lady intoned, "and I need your help pastor." For the sake of privacy, we will call her Marie. The call came from Brewton, Alabama. My wife, Joy, and I were casually acquainted with this lady and her husband.

Marie's story is like something out of a science fiction magazine or an Outer Limits television episode. Marie was committed to her church and ministered continually to others as a way of life.

One of these ministries was hospital visitation. Every patient in the town's small hospital received a weekly visit from this ardent believer in Jesus Christ. One of the patients in this facility was a very elderly man who was afflicted with severe and advanced rheumatoid arthritis. His joints were incredibly warped and twisted by this aggressive disease.

Circumstances around the onset of Marie's sickness were strange, eerie or bizarre. She just woke up one morning with throbbing joints. The prior afternoon, she had chanced to enter the hospital room of this arthritic patient just as he was dying. After praying with the grieving family, Marie left the hospital and headed home.

She would later testify that as soon as she got into her automobile that afternoon, a foul, putrid odor seemed to overwhelm her. The very next morning she awoke with her body wracked by pain.

Her doctor related that he had never seen a person so suddenly devastated by rheumatoid arthritis. The medical prognosis was grim. It was as though she was suddenly in the crosshairs of the grim reaper.

Marie had some very troubling questions. Could her condition have anything to do with the old gentleman whose death she had witnessed? Can an evil spirit cause some cases of arthritis? Could her sudden sickness have a connection to the awful smell in her car? Could the "rotten egg" smell actually have been an unclean spirit?

Marie posed all these questions to me. It was and is my conviction that "yes" is the answer to each of her questions. Marie then requested that Joy and I drive to Brewton and minister to her. As soon as possible was my answer to the anxious lady.

Marie's doctor emphatically told her that her condition was incurable and irreversible. The difficulty that she was experiencing would gradually intensify in every way; she was counseled by the medical profession.

When the Bible is taken at "face value," new and magnificent horizons open before us. Nothing becomes impossible for those who view the Bible as literally true. In Luke 13:10, there is a profoundly tantalizing story about a woman who suffered from a serious physical impairment for eighteen years. The cause of her ailment is both interesting and astonishing.

The King James Bible says that the woman had a "spirit of infirmity". Most of us cut our teeth on this particular translation. The problem is, however, that the majority of folks miss the truth here because the wording of the phrase makes the truth nebulous.

The New American Standard Bible reads that the "woman had a sickness caused by a spirit." The Amplified Bible says that the "woman had an infirmity caused by a spirit (a demon of sickness)."

Note that a spirit is a personality. A spirit that causes sickness and disease is evil. This does not indicate that the woman was evil; it indicates that an evil force attacked her.

Marie actually called us because she became highly suspicious that a force of darkness had invaded her. Joy and I made the three-hour trip because we knew that God would help this lady.

Upon arrival, I interviewed Marie. I was convinced that she was, indeed, a Christian. There was clear evidence that she was endeavoring to live a Christ-centered life. We did discover that Marie was struggling with several issues from childhood that remained unresolved.

I then commanded the trespassing spirit to identify itself. A growling voice spoke and declared, "I am the spirit that caused rheumatoid arthritis, and you cannot make me leave."

In Matthew 10:1, Jesus Christ clearly gives us the right to exercise power over every dark spirit. Joy and I both ordered this spirit to depart in the name of Jesus Christ.

This divine encounter took place about eighteen years ago. Marie has been free from arthritis since that magnificent day. The reader should understand that this lady's experience is highly unusual and should certainly not be looked upon as any kind of norm.

However, when a verifiable medical cause of sickness cannot be identified, the possibility of a dark spirit's presence should be entertained. To God be the glory for victory in this incredible encounter.

Two Miracles at a Mental Facility

Pastor Curtis called and asked me to minister to one of his church members confined to a mental health institution. I responded with my concern about the freedom to share under conditions that are possibly monitored by hospital staff. He assured me that the family would orchestrate a situation that would assure privacy for a confidential sharing time.

The patient's name was Joe. He had voluntarily checked himself into the facility seeking help for a serious personality problem. The incarcerated man acknowledged that for years anger had been out of control in his life.

The day that Joe entered the hospital, his anger had become a huge and ugly monster. In a blind rage, he had almost crossed a line of no return. In a state of passionate hostility, the troubled man had threatened to kill a family member with a long butcher knife.

When the crisis passed, Joe had no memory of the particulars of what had just happened. All he knew was that when he came to himself, he was pinning a loved one to the kitchen wall with an enormous knife. On the privacy of a bench under a huge, luscious and beautiful Magnolia tree, my new friend shared his agony with me. For most of his life, anger had become an increasingly more possessive monster. Now, it was threatening to devour him and maim the entire family permanently.

Joe related that when anger surged in his heart, a magnificent euphoria engulfed him temporarily. However, when the anger waned and passed, he would feel incredibly unclean and remorseful.

My new friend realized that he had offended God as well as his family. He prayed and asked God to forgive him for this ugly sin and set him free. It was obvious that he was in bondage to a dark spirit. "Help me," Joe pleaded.

As we sat quietly on that bench, I simply exercised authority over the spirit of anger present in Joe's life. The hideous thing had no choice but to depart. The very next day, Joe's doctor declared him "well." Joe was quickly released from the institution.

A year later, we were in a revival meeting at our church, when a stranger stood up and requested permission to give a testimony. This person asked, "Pastor, do you know who I am?"

My answer was to him was "no." The man proceeded to share that his name was Joe, and he was the man I ministered to on the hospital grounds the previous year.

"Thank you pastor," said Joe, "I am still a free man."

Some ten years later, a retired hospital employee told me that a nurse was dispatched to send me away as I ministered to the patient under that massive tree. This state hospital emissary reported that she could not approach me closer than fifty feet. It seemed to her that there was an invisible shield between the three of us, beyond which she could not pass.

When this was related to me, I then remembered seeing in my peripheral vision, a lady in a white uniform coming directly toward us, but stopping some distance away. Now we know the rest of the beautiful story. Two magnificent miracles occurred that day on the grounds of that hospital for disturbed souls.

God Heals Lady Who Lived in a Cage

This scene is forever etched in my memory. I remember the lady confined in a cage like a dangerous animal. Her habitat was a box about five feet square. The sides and back were made of solid concrete. The front consisted of huge iron bars in the form of a door. The only way out was the mercy of God.

This unforgettable experience took place in the vast interior of Central America's Guatemala. This ancient, regal, yet rustic city is Momostenango. Danny, Curtis and I were in this incredibly beautiful country to share the love of Jesus Christ.

I was handing out gospel tracts when our leader, Danny, sent for me. He had been preaching in the city's large prison when he became aware of the presence of a most unusual prisoner. This inmate was in the female section of the compound.

Prison officials, incredibly enough, inquired of the American evangelist if perhaps the female prisoner might receive some attention from our group. Her incarceration was not due to any crime against the State. It was more for her protection than anything else. The officials in question are praiseworthy for seeking aid for one who appeared to be absolutely beyond any help.

We never knew her real name. We will simply call her Juanita Doe. I reiterate that she was, indeed, incarcerated solely to protect her from something raging in her soul. This woman was horribly scarred from self-inflicted wounds.

Her attire was a plain, simple, sleeveless dress that stopped about four inches above her knees. The dress was tattered and much stained. More than likely she had worn it for a very sustained period of time.

Not even two-inches of visible flesh were free from hideous scars. Her skin was a mass of mutilation everywhere, including her face and neck.

Juanita's eyes revealed despair and intense fear. As we approached her cage, the woman was obviously very wary of our intentions. Danny addressed the woman in Spanish, which was her native tongue. My friend is quite fluent, as he preaches and ministers in this language. He explained to the bewildered prisoner our intentions and assured her that the officials had requested that we come and share God's love with her.

He further shared that I was going to pray and ask Jesus Christ to set her free from the darkness that was attempting to destroy her. As I prayed, Danny interpreted my words so Juanita would understand our true concern for her and grasp our heart's cry for her.

As I poured out my heart to God in her behalf, Juanita wept profusely. It was obvious that she was touched by our concern and by the love of God.

I fervently implored my Father God to set her free in the name of Jesus Christ. I commanded Dark spirits to loose her and be gone! Danny and I sensed that God had done a significant work in the caged woman. We left with a promise to return later in the day.

As night approached, we returned to Juanita's revolting cell. It was empty. The guard in charge explained that she had been transferred to the hospital for observation. With haste, we made our way to the city's only medical facility.

The lady that we had dubbed as Juanita Doe was not a patient in the facility. The head nurse explained that after examining the patient, the doctor declared Juanita to be of sound mind and body. Ms. Doe had been sent home, where she now belonged.

It has often been said that, "God is bigger than any mountain." I am still awed at the goodness and power of our Lord when I think of the lady that was made whole while in a cage. I will be looking forward to seeing her in heaven.

Dark Spirits Incredibly Vanquished

Being harassed is always a very unpleasant experience. At the root of this issue is always an evil spirit. The best way to deal with these situations is by utilizing the authority given to us by Jesus Christ, our Lord.

A conflict of this nature came to my attention several months ago. Angela and her husband, Todd, were the victims of this evil activity. The lady's uncle was the perpetrator of Angela and Todd's misery.

The obnoxious uncle lived next door to the couple. Horace, the uncle, is a homosexual who has the AIDS virus. Unk's disposition was as repulsive as his lifestyle.

This unsavory character was blatantly contentious. Horace would show up at his niece's home five to six times a day. In spite of his deviate choice of companionship, Unk constantly denigrated all the males in the family. Angela was especially bothered because Horace habitually targeted her husband above all others.

Todd and Angelia were Christians and had no desire to offend this physically and spiritually sick man. How could they, in good taste, end this nightmare? They requested that I pray with them about a peaceful solution to this volatile vexation.

The words of Jesus Christ in Matthew 10:1 rose up within me. Speaking to his disciples and to all believers as well, Christ said, "I give you authority over every evil spirit to expel them." The word authority here means "the right to exercise power".

I called the couple and shared with them a plan of action. I encouraged Angela and Todd to do the following things: Make sure that the confessions of their sins were to date. Make a thorough search of their home to remove any spiritually toxic items. Examples possibly could be things such as music, videos or literature that is unwholesome.

Next, they were encouraged to go into every room in the house and command every dark spirit to leave in the name of Jesus Christ. They were then encouraged to dedicate the house and all their possessions to God.

I instructed Todd and Angela to walk around the yard and follow the same regimen as they did inside the house. Additionally, the couple requested that the Holy Spirit of God stop any further harassment from Horace.

Angela recently called to share that the result of their spiritual warfare effort was quite remarkable. Only twice in three months had the uncle come near their home. Once he came and left a magazine on their front doorsteps and another time he just stuck his head in the front door, spoke and hastily departed.

About a month later, he suddenly moved to the Gulf Coast. This he did without sharing his plans with the couple.

"Do you consider this a miracle?" I asked Angela.

"Absolutely. There is no doubt about it. Everything is better in our entire life," she firmly stated. Todd came by a few days later and concurred with everything that his wife had shared with me.

Prominent Christian Leader Set Free

Many outstanding Christians struggle with bondages. Sometimes these battles rage for many years. The good news is that Jesus Christ came to set free all those brought into captivity by the enemy. This promise is clearly stated in Luke 4:19.

Will is a leader in his denomination. He is highly regarded and respected by his peers everywhere. Those who know him best are pleased with him. There was a time, however, when he was not very happy with himself.

Some years ago, Will requested an opportunity to converse with me. Upon his arrival, he quickly declared that he had a problem. "Nothing that I learned in school has prepared me to deal with this battle. I am a graduate of Mississippi College and the New Orleans Baptist Theological Seminary and still am not equipped to deal with this issue," declared the distraught minister.

"Every morning I pray for an hour and half," he related. With great sadness he added, "After all that praying, I can and often do have a temper tantrum fifteen minutes later. Can you help me?" he pleaded. I responded quietly and gently saying, "Jesus Christ can and will help you."

I informed my friend that he was under siege by a spirit of anger. Will had been in bondage to what Jesus called a "strong man."

This long-time minister was a precious man of God, but he had no concept of spiritual warfare. He was, however, both contrite and repentant.

He gave me permission to take authority over the dark spirit of anger that had brought him into perpetual defeat. In the name of Jesus Christ, I took authority over this foul spirit. Will was set free and has remained so for many years now. To our Christ belongs all honor and glory.

An Unexpected Evil Assault

Jesus Christ encountered dark spirits in ways that are seldom seen by the church today. There are several accounts in the New Testament in which unclean spirits seized people and threw them to the ground. For example, in Mark 19 an aggressive spirit of darkness assaulted an individual. I have witnessed similar activities several times.

The example cited here involved a person who was a pastor in a community some thirty miles from Meridian, Mississippi. This surprising and remarkable event was very similar to numerous Biblical happenings.

A very promising young pastor was the focus of a marauding spirit's attack. This dear, troubled pastor just showed up at my home unannounced and unexpected.

My wife was using my church office at that precise time to counsel a female member of our fellowship. It was, therefore, necessary for me minister to my friend in a Sunday school room.

A dark spirit began to manifest in the preacher as soon as our conversation began. Immediately, I began to authoritatively speak to the intruder in the young man's life. From a seated position, the subject was lifted up and thrown over two rows of chairs and against a wall.

However, my minister brother suffered no physical harm. This graphic display was a parting effort by the enemy to bring great harm to this Godly person.

The pastor in question has gone on to become an extremely effective servant of our great God. Set free, this godly man is now maturing into the spiritual general ordained by God as his destiny.

An Evil Spirit challenges pastor

The power display by Jesus Christ was greater than the manifestation of darkness. Actually, the greater assault was against the foul spirit that was vanquished for good that day.

Lies and deception are the main instruments of Satan's mode of operation. He also is very aggressive and boisterous as he confronts God's people. The element of surprise is also often utilized to shock and terrorize his victims.

An unexpected challenge was hurled at me as I ministered at a Christian rehabilitation facility. A deep voice came from the subject, accompanied by terrifying growling. Snarling menacingly, the voice challenged me with the question, "Jesus, I know, and Paul, I know, but who are you?"

Forcefully, I responded with a declaration of truth. "You foul spirit. I am a child of God, I have been washed in the blood of Jesus Christ and I am covered by His blood. Furthermore, I am filled with the Holy Spirit."

I continued by saying, "When you look at me, therefore, it is the same as looking at Jesus. Now be gone!" The dark spirit was immediately vanquished. The peace of God washed over this one who had been tormented. He was, indeed, free at last.

Mom Declares Wall Posters Were Possessed

Some would say that this is impossible. Consider the evidence and decide for yourself.

A teenage girl is the subject of this particular scenario. Posters of Young adults' pictures who had achieved fame as somewhat radical musicians decorated the teen's bedroom walls. The Holy Spirit had recently touched both her parents in a powerful way. When this experience took place, the church where this family worshipped was in a revival meeting,

On the night in question, the evangelist targeted the youth in his preaching effort. He had endeavored to warn his audience to the dangers of certain kinds of music. The speaker had even cautioned that inappropriate wall posters could be spiritually dangerous.

Back home, after church, the mother asked her daughter to get the controversial posters out of the house. A major family conflict over the issue then erupted. The hour was late, and the family was tired as they faced getting up early for work and school.

However, a compromise negotiated. The offending posters were to be removed from sight. The daughter decided to store them underneath her bed.

Immediately, the bed began to move and shake like it was alive. The daughter freaked out and ran screaming for her mother. Great alarm gripped everyone in the house.

The daughter, along with both her mom and dad, very quickly gathered up the possessed posters and got them out of the house. The family did not breathe a sigh of relief until the items were carefully and prayerfully burned in the back yard.

This was the end of the problem. I stress that dark spirits can inhabit inanimate objects. Families who are having unusual and unexplained problems in the home should do a thorough search of their entire premises.

Remove and destroy all suspicious items. The house and land should then be prayed over and deliberately dedicated to God anew and afresh.

Man Is Delivered from Twelve Demons

Twelve distinctly different voices spoke through James as he writhed on the floor. He had come to my office under duress. Crystal, his fiancée, had driven him to our home on this occasion. He had been adamantly opposed to coming, but the fiancée told James, "The wedding is off, if you do not see Pastor Jack."

Jim, as he was called, was sitting in front of a large bookcase as I began to inquire about what made his visit necessary. When they arrived at our home, the young man had refused to get out of the car. I went out and basically ordered him to come in. What happened next absolutely caught me by surprise.

All of a sudden, it was as if a force threw him backward into my books and onto the floor. Books went in every direction. His body contorted as he alternately and violently pulled at his hair and/or his shirt. Alien voices poured forth from his throat.

To protect Jim from harming himself, I leaped on him as a man rides a horse. With strength provided by my Lord, I pinned both of his arms to the floor as he intensely resisted. A deep voice growled and declared, "I hate this sucker, and I have tried to kill him twice lately."

The first such experience happened where Jim was employed. He had gone into the attic of the building to retrieve an item that was stored there. He was squatting down to look at something when he temporarily forgot that the ceiling was lower than normal. In a hurry, Jim, got up quickly and butted his head against a steel beam.

He was knocked out as cold as a cucumber by the trauma. An ambulance carried him to Anderson's Regional Medical Center. He was in the emergency room for at least six hours. During most of this time, James was unconscious. I, along with my wife and Crystal, were with him most of the time.

Intermittently he would wake up and quickly go out again. The strange thing was that the doctors could find no reason for what was happening. As the day wore on, there was some talk of exploratory surgery on his head. All of us were praying almost constantly for Jim.

Suddenly he woke up and said, "I'm fine now." Somewhat confused by the entire episode, the doctors dismissed the patient. Even then, we believed that the devil had tried to kill our friend.

The second accident was a few days before they came to see me. James had stepped on a nail, which pierced all the way through his foot. This could have been a very serious problem, but by the grace of God, it was not. He was still limping when they arrived on the day of these demonic manifestations.

My wife, Joy, and Crystal were in another room praying when a harsh, rasping voice cried, "Listen to those silly women. They are praying against us." The ladies were absolutely too far away to have been understood by natural hearing.

The dark spirits, however, clearly knew and understood what was taking place. When each new voice spoke with claims of owning James, I rebuked and commanded it to leave in the name of Jesus Christ. The entire traumatic encounter lasted for two hours, but God the Almighty set Jim free that day.

Windows of the Soul

The eyes of a person are the windows to their soul. God often utilizes one's eyes to expose or reveal things long hidden deep within them. The experience that I now share is a remarkable example of God's creative ability to enlighten in this manner.

God's agenda here was more than just to inform, but the ultimate purpose was to set free one of his children. The lady sitting before me had been in bondage for a very long time. Her life had been in disarray since childhood. Hope sprang up within her now because of what God had recently done in her husband's life.

Jack had been radically touched and set free the night before in my office. The entire family knew that something beautiful and magnificent had transpired within him. Now, Nell had come seeking her own miracle.

I interviewed the lady in an attempt to discover the root cause of her problem. We conversed at length as she shared her own agony. The origin of her problems eluded our perception or understanding.

At this point, I asked for permission to stare into her eyes to seek revelation from God. I expected disclosure to be regarding those things hidden in her soul. What happened was absolutely mindboggling.

After several minutes, Nell gasped, "Oh, my God, your eyes are like a television screen. I can see something happening to me when I was eight years old." Nell sobbed deeply, "Now I know why I have been hurting all these years."

After regaining her composure, Nell was able to forgive her abuser. Afterwards, as I prayed, the astonished lady's heart was healed and at last she found peace. The windows of a person's soul are powerful allies in discovering truth.

The Cross is a Symbol of Victory

Status in society has nothing to with humanity's struggles with darkness. The affluent and cultured or the exact opposite all have similar challenges. Robin was a cool, coiffured lady whose heart condition startled both me and my wife, Joy.

We were praying with Robin when the manifestation occurred. She began to cackle loudly and boldly, like something out of an old horror movie. The foul thing began to taunt me, declaring that it could not be forced to leave. Nothing that I said seemed to threaten the ugly, dark spirit.

I was sitting in a chair facing Robin as these activities commenced. Suddenly she began to cringe and wave her arms in a defensive posture. The same shrill, high-pitched voice again came out of Robin crying, "No, no, no, stop it, stop it, don't do that. Get it away from me."

Astonished, I looked around to see what was happening. Joy had a twelve-inch wooden cross in her right hand. She was waving this symbol of authority menacingly toward the heckling voice that proceeded from our guest.

The dark force in Robin was repelled for good by the symbol of power that my wife utilized on that critical occasion. The lady wept and gained her composure after this battle was won in a most unexpected way.

The Cross brought about this significant victory. Furthermore, at times like this, it is always helpful to sing songs about the Blood of Jesus. Often we have sung these songs repeatedly because the enemy is vanquished by the power of the Blood and the name of Jesus.

An Unusual Manifestation of Darkness

Paul Billheimer, a noted Christian author, once wrote that he believes that when we get to heaven, we will discover that a surprising amount of our problems are caused by dark spirits.

Jesus said the evil one comes only to steal, kill and destroy. Our enemy exercises a great deal of ingenuity in his war against the saints.

Such was the case of Tabitha. She was an incredibility fine Christian lady. One of the ministries that God had given to her was that of pianist in her church.

Additionally, she was a prayer warrior. Playing the piano as part of the Sunday worship, however, was the great love of her life.

Tabitha knew about our ministry of helping hurting people. She, therefore, called and requested that we meet with her and two of her friends. An appointment was scheduled for these troubled people.

We were able to be God's instruments in helping these friends of Tab's. As this session concluded, she asked if she might share a problem of her own with us.

She was encountering a distinct and peculiar difficulty. Each time she began to play the piano at church, her chin would begin to swell noticeably. The problem was so intense that Tab found it necessary to avoid the piano at church.

The lady was not the victim of an allergy. A "spirit of infirmity," as noted in Luke 10:11, was attacking Tab. Standing on the Scripture Matthew 10:1, we exercised authority on Tabitha's behalf. The swelling never occurred again, even when she played the church piano.

Pastor Set Free from Unclean Spirit

Pastor David and I were friends. We had ministered together many times. "I need help with a long standing problem," he confided after a Bible study one night. The occasion was what Baptists call January Bible Study.

"I have this nagging pain between my shoulder blades, and it's been there a long time," declared the young pastor. "No remedy that I have tried has succeeded in eliminating my anguish. It just will not go away!"

David requested that I pray for him. We were both in for a monumental surprise. After some discussion about the perplexing complaint, I realized that his pain did not have an organic origin. An unusual experience in the Bible seemed to fit David's trauma.

In the Bible's book of Luke, Chapter 13, there is chronicled the story of a woman who had a sickness caused by an evil spirit. This was obviously the case with this pastor. The subsequent events validated my grim diagnosis.

Looking into David's eyes, I began to tell the spirit of darkness to leave. A moaning began to come from deep within David, and his face turned an ashen gray. The unearthly sound became so intense that I became concerned for the life of my friend.

With a God-imparted surge of faith, I held David's head between my hands and forcefully took authority over the trespassing dark spirit. I aggressively commanded, "Come out of him you foul spirit, in Jesus Name!"

Instantly there was an ear-piercing scream as the pastor crumpled to the floor. Simultaneously, the family's dog went absolutely bananas just outside the house. I thought, "My Lord, is David dead?"

As quickly as David had fallen, he sprang to his feet shouting, "I am healed, I am healed, praise God." At the same time, I thought he was going to hug me to death as he ecstatically celebrated his supernatural healing.

It is my conviction that the departing evil spirit entered the family's dog. A fantastic release of the power of God had set a captive free. Such experiences should be normal fare for Kingdom people.

Porn under the Mattress

A lack of understanding abounds concerning the relationship between dark spirits and those whom they inhabit. Spirits refer to a person as "their house." They hate the person whose body they have invaded.

This is clearly communicated in Bob's experience. He was a teenager referred to us for help. Inquiry time disclosed the problem to be pornographic in nature. Embarrassed, the youth said that he wanted to be free from this unwholesome activity. As the spiritual cleansing process commenced, several additional issues surfaced.

As we began to deal with the array of dark spirits by addressing the spirit of pornography, an unexpected interruption occurred. A voice declared accusingly, "He does not want to be free, because there is porn hidden under his mattress." I immediately stopped the process.

Bob admitted to being unwittingly exposed. He confessed his deception and repented to God. This was a time of victory for the entire family.

With the porn spirit extricated, the youth made a commitment to burn the lurid material. This experience was a new and wonderfully good beginning for Bob.

Haunted House in West Texas

The house sitter adamantly declared that she would not go back in that house. Her job was in jeopardy, yet the unexplained mysterious manifestations in her workplace terrorized her. The homeowners were away for an extended period, and the sole responsibility of the edifice was in her hands.

Almost every day there appeared eerie and strange phenomenon in various rooms of the house. These appearances took the form of lights that materialized and vanished in a sporadic manner. After these appearances left, what was described as an eyeball would manifest and menacingly move around the room in the air before vanishing.

My sister, Willie recounted the story to us. She was a friend of the embattled house sitter. We were spending some vacation time in the city when the concern was shared with us. "Could we deal with the issue?" we were asked. Our answer was "yes!" Willie, Joy and I met with the harried sitter at the troubled house. We went into every room in the dwelling, and in accordance with Matthew 10:1 verbally took authority over every evil spirit in the house. We commanded them in the name of Jesus Christ to leave and never to return. Their departure was, indeed, permanent. Later, word came that the weird and unusual sightings never returned. We were pleased, but the house sitter was ecstatic.

Who Was the Stranger?

"I will buy you a ticket for any place in the world that you would like to go," said the stoic stranger in a quiet, unemotional voice. Why would anyone make such a preposterous offer? What possible motive could have prompted such a proposition?

My wife and I had recently moved into the city of Meridian, Mississippi. God had led us to plant a new Christian Church. On this occasion, I was on an errand to the Bible Book Store. The nearest parking space was in front of a billiards parlor. The establishment was a forbidding-looking place. The windows were almost covered, and it appeared to be nearly dark inside.

There were two parking places available in front of the nefarious looking business. As I pulled into the first parking slot, two men emerged from the building. One man turned to his right and went up the sidewalk. The other individual moved toward the street as if he planned to cross to the other side.

The second man stopped in the empty parking space and faced me as I disembarked from my car. I was in a hurry and paid little attention as to how either of the men was dressed. As I stood up and closed the car door, the stranger was almost in my face. Looking directly into my eyes, this ominous person made an incredibly perplexing offer. I was so dumbfounded at his words that I was speechless. I moved toward the Bible Book Store while he just stood there staring toward me.

It is my conviction that a dark and sinister spirit spoke to me through one whom he was controlling that day. The words were a lame attempt to cause me to abort the agenda that God planned for me in the city. When I get to heaven, I will ask about the purpose of that strange man.

Scott and Tonya Dared to Dream Big!

Almost all great achievements in exploration, science and technology began in the heart of someone who had a dream. Not only did Scott and Tonya dream big, but they dared to indefatigably pursue the passion of their heart.

Wernher von Braun is a classic example. He was a leading figure in the development of rocket technology. Much of his accomplishments as a scientist were birthed in his heart as a teenager.

Countless adults who are living mediocre lives are folks who once had big dreams. In their view, they lost these dreams because of some unfortunate circumstance. Pursuit of a dream often involves some measure of risk. Risk always breeds some degree of fear.

People do not just lose their dream. Satan steals dreams from folks whenever possible. It is the conviction of this writer that God puts dreams in the heart of his beloved.

I am further convinced that your God-given destiny is the dream that you have long cherished. You are encouraged to resurrect your dream and pursue it with abandonment of fear.

Scott and Tonya were an outstanding Christian couple who were an integral part of our church family. Even before they became husband and wife, their hearts were pregnant with dreams from God. Scott's passion was to become a Mechanical Engineer. Tonya wanted to own her own business.

Providentially, they fell in love and were married. Soon along came beautiful Hannah. Scott was enrolled in Mississippi State University in Starkville, Mississippi, at that time of their wedding.

About halfway through the degree program, responsibility became more extensive. Scott dropped out of college and went to work for his dad.

The scenario that developed did not lessen their love for each other or for their Lord. They were in church up to their eyeballs and contributed effectively to the total program.

Their lives seemed to be full and complete until one Sunday morning they were jolted to a new awareness. I preached on "Daring to Pursue Your Dream."

Scott and Tonya's dreams reawakened that fateful Lord's Day morning. The couple did not stutter, dawdle or hesitate. They prayed, and God reaffirmed that their dreams had indeed come from Him.

Tonya began to pursue her dream. She started a children's recycled clothing store. She called her new business Pappyhat's Trunk. This venture was successful; the business helped them survive financially during the lean time of Scott's schooling, and it provided much satisfaction to Tonya.

This precious couple was willing to bite the bullet in every way necessary for Scott to re-enroll in the university. Never for one moment have they doubted their decision in this matter.

As steadily as the swinging of the pendulum on a metronome, Scott methodically met every challenge in the process of his quest. It has now been seventeen years since he was awarded a degree in Mechanical Engineering.

Scott, Tonya and Hannah have been living out their dream in North Carolina all these years. Their dreams almost slipped away, but in the nick of time, they boldly seized them again and never let go.

Perhaps someone who reads these lines needs to resurrect his or her own long lost dream. In this event, it will certainly be important to spend much time with the dream-giver.

It may be necessary to go back to school or begin preparation in some other way. Remember, a godly dream is planted in your heart by your loving Father God. His dream for you is your destiny. Will you dare to begin now to do the impossible with His help?

God Works in Mysterious Ways

My friend Andrew recently received a healing. The manner in which this happened was somewhat unusual. Miracles are always magnificent, however they manifest.

This incident demonstrated the sovereign grace of a loving and merciful God. It does indicate that Father God often works in unique and unusually interesting ways.

Andrew had been struggling in several areas in recent weeks. Because of these challenges, I called to encourage and pray for him almost every day.

On a call a couple of weeks ago, Andy indicated that he was experiencing a great deal of rather acute pain. He had no idea what might be causing this difficulty.

In my prayer for Andrew, I rebuked his pain. I also took authority over the root cause of the discomfort. Next, I thanked God for taking care of my friend's problem.

About twenty-four hours later, Andy called me back. He thanked me for praying and proceeded to tell me that God had answered my prayer.

He also shared with me that immediately after I finished praying, something unusual transpired.

He emptied from his bladder four large kidney stones. He had not even realized that he had these stones.

Again, he said, "Thank you, Bro. Jack; God really did hear your prayers."

I have reached a place in my life where my prayers have changed. In the Amplified Bible, Hebrews 4:16, God declares we should approach the throne of grace "fearlessly, confidently and boldly."

I encourage you to check out this excellent study Bible. You will be blessed by this version.

Darlene Shares some Family Miracles

Miracles have abounded in the Whittington household. "The following are just a few that have been a part of our lives," Darlene shares.

In 1982, I was stricken with an illness that began with a violent headache that was so severe my ears were affected seriously. My hearing was impaired, and a sound like crinkling tinfoil was constantly in my ears. I didn't go to the doctor because I thought I had a flu-type virus. There was a virus going around that people said began with very bad head pain. I took pain medication every four hours and slept most of the time.

After a week or so, I went to the doctor because I still had symptoms; my balance and hearing were affected. He felt I had viral encephalitis. From that point on, every month or two, I had a migraine-type headache that would incapacitate me for approximately 50 hours.

When we moved to Meridian in 1987, I was still having these severe headaches. We began attending Church of the Way, and I saw people coming forward to the altar for prayer for healing. My faith increased. Soon, I went forward one Sunday, and Brother Jack prayed for me. Often in his messages he would say, "If you don't receive healing instantly, continue coming for prayer for your healing."

It took several years, but as I received prayer the headaches began to get further and further apart. One day they were gone, and I never had another one. I could tell the difference between these headaches and an ordinary headache. God healed me of these horrible headaches. He took them completely away.

I also want to tell of another miraculous healing I received. An unusual spot appeared on my right cheekbone close to my eye. I began putting my hand over the problem area as I prayed. I got Brother Jack and Mrs. Joy and others to pray for me. The spot became so bad and so unsightly I wore a band-aid over it. People would ask me about it, and if I showed them, most would say, "You need to see a doctor."

I felt in my spirit God wanted to heal this place, so I never went to the doctor. It was large and covered with red, bloody spots. One day the edges of this lesion began to come loose and had begun to get very dry. It fell off my cheek, leaving nothing–no mark, no scar, no sign whatever and the skin where it had been was flawless.

A similar situation happened to my husband. A bump grew in front of one of his ears. It was crusty and bled quite a bit. We prayed over it, commanding it to go in Jesus' name. It dried up and fell off.

Another exciting miracle that happened to him took place in approximately 1994. He was having excruciating stomach pain. After seeing our doctor, Sam was hospitalized. When tests showed gallstones, surgery was scheduled.

On a Wednesday night after prayer meeting, a couple who attended our church was going home. They were passing the hospital, having just prayed for Sam in the prayer group at church. They felt the Lord speaking to them to stop and see him and pray with the laying on of hands for him.

Because of the lateness of the hour being around 8:30 p.m., the couple hesitated to enter the hospital. However, the prompting of the Lord was strong, so they obeyed and went into Sam's room. As they prayed over him, Sam felt the power of God come upon him. The next day he told his doctor he wasn't going to have the surgery. He was going to go home, but if he wasn't healed, he would make arrangements to have surgery later.

Sam never had the surgery. Furthermore, he has never had any more problems with his gallbladder.

Obedience: the Key to God's Blessings

God makes this truth clear through various Bible passages. A prime example of this indisputable teaching is in the Bible's book of I Samuel. The Lord declared through his prophet, "It is better to obey God than to present a sacrifice to Him" (22:15).

God removed King Saul from his ruling position because of his dismal failure in the matter of obedience. Obviously, obedience is a matter of paramount importance to God.

Recently, God taught this truth to a fellow pastor and at the same time provided a new friend for me. We will call him Len, in the interest of privacy. This well-known minister of the gospel has been the pastor of an area church for more than ten years. His reputation is impeccable. Until he came into my office one day, his face was unknown to me.

He began by telling me that two weeks prior to this moment, God had spoken to him as he drove past our church. The Lord said something to the effect, "Stop at this church and meet the pastor."

Len continued, "I just kept right on driving, but today I have come to be obedient. I don't know what this is all about; I just know that I now had to obey God" For more than an hour we each shared much about our spiritual journey over the years.

Len and I ended the time of sharing by praying together. My new friend suggested that we share again one week later. This seemed good because we knew that God had an agenda. What it might be was unknown to both of us.

The next week our sharing experience lasted for an hour and a half. Again, we prayed one for the other before he departed. Once more we pledged to meet for prayer the following Friday morning at 10:30 a.m.

I received a call from Len the next Friday morning at about 8:30. An emergency had arisen, and he would not be able to meet with me that day.

During this conversation, Len said with a tinge of excitement in his voice, "Bro. Jack, I have something very important to share with you.

As you prayed for me last week, God broke something off of me that I sense had been there a long time. As I got in my truck to leave, I realized that something significant had happened in my life."

I had prayed by the direction of the Holy Spirit for my esteemed friend. God had heard and moved him a bit closer to his divine destiny.

That is, God elevated Len to a new place in the Kingdom of God that day, made possible because two weeks earlier he had obeyed God in a matter that was of little sense to his human understanding. Actually, Len had passed a crucial test in this matter of obedience. He, therefore, was in a position to receive a promotion by his pleased heavenly Father.

Each of us at some point will face an opportunity to stay where we are or to take a giant step toward our destiny. Spiritual advancement hinges obedience to a word from our Lord. This word will likely come in the form of a gentle prompting by the Holy Spirit. Your destiny hangs on simply obeying that word.

The Danger of Saying No to God

As I entered Ed's room he was cursing and ranting. He lay in a fetal position in the hospital bed. He was unshaven, his hair disheveled and his eyes were wild. I called him by name, and he turned his face toward me.

The patient looked a lot older than he really was. Alcoholism had consumed his adult life. When sober, he was a hard worker and a nice guy. When I first met Ed, it was obvious that his meager possessions gave mute testimony to a wasted life.

He and his wife, Effie, owned and operated an incredibly small country store. Almost forever, to supplement their income, Ed had made runs to the Mississippi Gulf Coast to buy shrimp and fish. His dependability in this business earned a good number of regular customers.

The couple's store was on the edge of our church community. I would often stop and talk with them while sipping an ice cold drink. Effie shared with me that early in life she had given her heart to Jesus Christ. Ed would not talk about the matter, but affirmed that he was not a Christian.

On a routine visit, I found that Ed was not in his store. His wife declared that he was a very sick man. I asked for permission to go in and pray for him. Upon entering the bedroom, I discovered that Ed had his face to the wall in the very corner of the antiquated room.

I paused at the foot of the rickety old bed, but he did not stir or acknowledge my presence. After a few awkward minutes, I very gently asked, "Can I talk with you?"

"Yeah, preacher, I don't mind," he uttered in almost a whisper.

The bed was really close to the wall, so talking with him face to face was not a simple matter. As I gingerly made my way through the narrow space, I found myself wading through dozens of empty beer cans.

I carefully knelt among the empty containers and shared the message of Jesus Christ with Ed one more time. "I'm ready now, preacher," he said, with a sound of relief in his voice.

Ed acknowledged to God that his heart was empty and that his life was without purpose. "Come into my heart and forgive my sins," he cried to God.

Amazingly, Ed got well very quickly. His family rejoiced with him over the decision to receive Jesus Christ as his Savior.

The new Christian was gently implored to attend church and to make a public confession of his faith in Christ. Ed readily agreed to go to church the next Sunday. The entire church fellowship warmly welcomed him and his wife, Effie. To our sorrow, the new convert would not attend another worship service.

A few weeks later, Effie called to say that Ed was, in her words, "a mighty sick man." He was in Jeff Anderson Hospital. "Will you come and pray for him, pastor?" she pleaded. "But I need to warn you," she continued, "He's cussin' everybody that comes into the room." I assured her that I would be there quickly.

When I got within fifty feet of the hospital room, I could hear his tirade. Effie cautiously ushered me into the room. His language was abusive until he realized that I was the pastor.

"Pastor, I am glad you came. I need to tell you something," he said as if to measure his words. "You remember when you came to our house and prayed with me? Well, that was real. I was really saved that day. I knew that God wanted me to go to church and get baptized, but I refused. What you see now is the result of my saying no to God."

Ed's eyes blinked and something sinister stared at me. The friend that had just spoken to me seemed to be gone now. His heart quit beating a few days later. I was literally shaken by what I had experienced in that hospital room. Disobedience had opened Ed's heart to a dark and destructive presence.

Black Lab Alerts Couple of Danger

It is true that God works in mysterious ways His wonders to perform. Our house averted a tragic fire a few nights ago because of this verity. Our Lord caused an incredible thing to happen in our midst.

At the center of this amazing experience is a beautiful, black Labrador retriever. His name is Rocky, and he belongs to our son, Mark. This regal canine is about a year and a half old.

We normally keep Rocky in the garage at night. The reason for his being there is twofold. The first is simply that we wanted to keep him inside and out of the cold weather. Secondly, he usually barks too much when he has the run of the yard at night.

Three nights ago, I called Mark's dog in and let the door down at precisely 10:00 p.m. I promptly went to bed and soon was fast asleep.

At 12:00 p.m., Rocky woke me up, barking like crazy. I endured this barrage until it was obvious that the tirade was more than I could tolerate.

With the delightful prospect of sleeping again soon, I traipsed to the halls outside door. Opening the door to the garage, I reached out and bumped the switch that would raise the big door. To my surprise, nothing happened. Fully awake now, and half-frustrated, I punched the button again. The result was the same as before.

About that time, I realized that my nostrils were being assaulted by an extremely acrid odor. It smelled as if rubber was on fire. I then hastened to open the roll-down door manually. It absolutely would not budge. Rocky's stress level elevated to a much higher level by this time. I quickly hatched another plot to get him out of the garage. I decided to lead him through the kitchen and on out through the great room.

He would have none of this endeavor. Numerous times he had tried to enter the house just because the door was cracked a bit. Not now, even though I was coaxing him with all my savvy. He actually ran when I attempted to get hold of his collar.

Had Rocky gone out through the house proper I might have ignored the smell and gone back to bed. However, I was now aggravated at the dog and the garage door, so I went looking for a ladder to try something else.

I climbed the ladder to eyeball the motor to see if I might discover a clue as to what to do next. Surrounding the motor that opens the garage door is a strong and stiff plastic covering.

I reached up and touched the outer covering; when I did, it moved slightly. The chain instantly shifted forward about four inches. Only then did I realize that the motor had been running for the past two hours and had been in great duress the entire time.

I then cautiously touched the top of the motor with my left index finger. The motor was hot beyond belief. My breath was almost taken away as my hand recoiled from the almost red-hot mechanism.

The slight moving of the chain relieved the stress from the door. I then was able to raise it manually. Rocky bounded into the fresh air and was surprisingly quiet for the rest of the night.

One of my electrician friends shared with me that the motor should have had a kill switch that cut the motor off when the chain snagged and created undue stress. It is, therefore, highly likely that a fire would soon have erupted had the condition not been discovered.

It is my conviction that my loving and gracious heavenly Father got involved and aborted an impending disaster. Our very lives quite possibly were saved in the process.

A Bible verse suggests that children are assigned guardian angels to watch over them (Matthew 18:10). Humanly speaking, I am an old guy, yet I am still His child. All things considered, it seems likely that all believers have angels assigned to them.

God really is our "daddy." Galatians 4:6 says that we may call Him "Abba," which is Aramaic for daddy, instead of father. Not only that, but He is the best daddy in the whole wide world.

A Social Security Miracle

Walter Earl was very, very angry and greatly distraught. He had a "proverbial" bomb dropped in his lap. This situation amounted to an absolute financial disaster.

Walter has been confined to a wheelchair for some years. He lives alone and subsists on social security benefits.

His prescription medicine bills are astronomical because of an array of serious health issues. Over the last several years, he has undergone several critical surgical procedures that were life threatening.

The "bomb" directed toward him was in the form of a blistering verbal message from a representative of the Social Security Administration.

The caller informed Walter that his check was being cut approximately 70 percent. My friend was told that the decision was not open for discussion or subject to any appeal.

The caller indicated that the reduction was a "done" deal. The repercussions of such a radical experience were traumatizing to Walter.

His call to me was for prayer. I prayed with him about this terrible injustice. I voiced my prayer according to the Amplified version of Hebrews 4:16. This particular rendering of the verse admonishes us to come to the "throne of grace," fearlessly, confidently and boldly.

Neither he nor I have any legal standing before any earthly court. However, we do have the right to come freely before Heaven's Supreme Court.

I appealed the matter to the Supreme Justice of the entire universe. I prayed in the manner prescribed in Hebrews.

Just two days later, the verdict was handed down. The entire matter, although adjudicated before, was now rendered null and void.

Walter Earl was ecstatic when he telephoned me. "God has answered your prayer," he bubbled. We both were careful to give the credit to God because only He could have achieved this magnificent thing.

Your every problem is subject to the authority of King Jesus. I urge you to begin to pray according to the Hebrews admonition of chapter 4:16. You will be glad.

Miracle in a Miami Hospital

God recently surprised us again with an incredible miracle. When something of great magnitude occurs, too often we are amazed, even though we have prayed for such a thing to happen. May God bring all of us to the place of eagerly expecting a grand and glorious answer to the cry of our heart.

Our friend, Denise, recently called with an urgent prayer request. She asked that I pray immediately and then to share their need with others who believe in miracles.

She explained that their oldest son, Michael, was critically ill in a Miami, Florida, hospital. The night before she called, he had experienced a heart attack. Family members on the scene informed her of the seriousness of the situation. The very moment that she called me, Michael was being prepared to have a heart catherization.

With Denise on the phone, I prayed fearlessly, confidently and boldly (Hebrews 4:16 Amplified version). When her call came in, I was helping a friend get his vehicle repaired; therefore, I was unable to contact anyone else for the next hour.

About the time that I got back to my office, Denise called again. This time she was ecstatic with good news. At this time, she had just conversed with the doctor who had performed the Cath procedure.

In this conversation, she related a bit more of the situation to me. The night before, when Michael entered the hospital's emergency room, his heart was beating only four times per minute. This, along with other diagnostic procedures, produced the heart attack conclusion.

The attending physician related to Denise that the catherization had been finished in a record amount of time. He now was confident from the Cath and other test results that there was absolutely no problem with Michael's heart.

The medical personnel did not understand what had transpired in the situation, but they were very encouraged by their final conclusion. Consequently, Michael was immediately discharged from the facility.

Denise said to me, "Pastor, I am absolutely amazed and dumbfounded at what God has done. I want to thank you for your prayers."

Musings on Exorcism

The Author's Exorcism Odyssey

The word exorcism is actually not found in the Bible. Webster's Dictionary says that it "means to get rid of something troublesome, menacing, or oppressive; such as an evil spirit." It may also refer to the actual calling out an evil spirit from an individual.

The word exorcism may refer to the act or practice of exorcising. This was very clearly a routine a part of the ministry of Jesus Christ, as he endeavored to set humanity free from bondage.

My involvement in this ministry was never something that I envisioned or deliberately pursued; rather, it seemed to evolve as a sovereign choice of Jehovah God. When helping people, God often surprises His people with the path on which He plants their feet.

God has honored my wife's and my obedience in this ministry in a remarkable way. It has been, by far, the most effective work in which God has used us over a span of many years.

This article is in no way an attempt to be exhaustive or scholarly on the subject of exorcism. Rather, it is a brief account of some of the experiences that my wife and I have encountered in our efforts to help hurting people.

We have been a part of several hundred very similar situations. Almost everyone involved has been a person in church leadership of some nature. Numerous of these individuals have been in full time Christian ministry.

The Bible was given to us by God over many centuries, yet it obviously has one author and a single theme. Because it is clearly God's Word, it will be relevant as long as the world remains.

Customs, cultures and languages change, but the needs of the human heart remain the same. God's answer to the cry of man also remains unchanged.

None sane among us would suggest that the nature of man has improved since Jesus returned to the Father. It is, therefore, obvious that needs addressed by Jesus, when he was on earth, remain disturbingly present in this chaotic culture.

When Jesus Christ walked among men, three things were at the heart of his ministry. He proclaimed the gospel of the Kingdom to bring men to salvation. He continually healed all manner of sick people. Additionally, delivering individuals from demonic control was a routine activity of the Christ.

As a youngster attending church, 100 percent of church focus was on the message of how to be saved. The sick were prayed for occasionally, but with zero expectation of supernatural healing. The possibility of present-day demonic activity among civilized Americans was never a consideration.

It is imperative we awaken to the truth that Jesus Christ transferred His entire agenda to the church. As we view the fields that are ripe unto harvest, it is crucial that we minister in the power of the Holy Spirit to all the needs that confront us.

The stories in this book are examples of our effort to fulfill the mandate of Jesus as stated in Matthew 28:18-20. Most folks miss a key issue in this command of our Lord.

According to this passage, everyone who receives salvation is to be taught to do all that Jesus commanded His disciples. Clearly, this means to preach the Gospel of the Kingdom, pray for the healing of the sick and to exercise authority over unclean spirits when such is the case.

Simple Truths about the Spirit World

A critically important observation about Satan or the Devil does not need to be overlooked: He is absolutely not omnipresent. This simply means that he is not everywhere at the same time. Though he can obviously change locations, his activity is confined to a particular place of his choice.

This being the case, you may ask why then is there so much evil everywhere? The simple truth is that Satan has so many helpers who endeavor to fulfill his agenda.

Some of these helpers are often called demons. At other times, they are referred to as unclean or foul spirits. According to Ephesians 6:11-

12, a distinct and evil hierarchal structure, whose specific purpose is to steal, kill and destroy, exists in this world

You and I are human beings. We basically exist in spirit form. This spirit called man lives in a house that we call a body. The man spirit also has a soul. The soul of man consists of a mind, will and emotions.

Understand: a "spirit" is a personality. Evil or unclean spirits are also personalities. Demons are, therefore, spirit. They bear similarity to the man spirit. That is, they can talk or communicate, as well as think and scheme (Ephesians 6:11).

Man's body is the vehicle through which his spirit communicates with others. The evil helpers of Satan do not have their own bodies. Their agenda, therefore, is to latch on to a human being. They can then speak through the human and use them to do the bidding of the great dragon (see Revelations 12:17).

The network of evil multiplies as oppressed people are controlled to various degrees by unclean spirits. It is profoundly interesting that dark spirits sometimes refer to human beings as "My house."

This is clearly shown in Matthew 12:43-44. I, along with my wife, have heard countless unclean spirits make this assertion exactly as stated in the above scripture.

You may ask why you have never heard an evil spirit speak. Again, the answer is very simple. They normally do not audibly speak unless they are extremely agitated, provoked or challenged.

Remaining quiet and seeking to be anonymous is greatly to their advantage. The believer should understand and rejoice that he absolutely does have the right to exercise power over such beings.

Understanding Your God Given Authority

In Matthew 10:1, Jesus gave His disciples authority over unclean spirits, to cast them out. Sadly and tragically, Many Christians are convinced that this authority was only for the original twelve.

Those of this persuasion should note that in Luke, Chapters 10-11, Jesus gives a similar command to at least seventy followers. Also in Mathew 28:19-20, all who believe are to be taught to observe everything that Jesus taught his disciples.

Only when the Bible is taken at face value can believers achieve the level of victory that is their destiny. Jesus assures us in John 10:10 that he came to give life that is full and complete.

To consistently live the abundant life, it is imperative that believers understand and utilize the power given to them. This truth is the intent of this essay.

The word "authority" in Matthew 10:1 means the right to "exercise power" over the unclean spirits. Jesus Christ is saying that we can do this if we choose to do so.

Many years ago a military aircraft crashed on some property owned by one of my friends. Authorities stationed a military policeman to guard the site against looters.

Sometime later, my friend related to me that curiosity seekers pilfered a major part of the wreckage. "Why did this guard allow this to happen?" I asked my friend.

His response to me was, "I suppose that he was young and did not know his authority." This answer was classic and is uniquely applicable to this present subject.

Please hear this again. Jesus gave you and me authority to exercise power over every unclean spirit. The question is, will we receive this authority and confidently use it over this adversary?

Again, I pose a crucial question to the reader. Where are the unclean spirits to which Jesus referenced? Most would say, "They are oppressing some bad dudes next door or down the block."

I am certain that Jesus was referencing some folks like this. However, many good folks who read these lines are certain to be doing battle with some form of darkness.

The warfare begins in the mind. Before a battle is lost in the flesh, it has already been lost in the mind. Our first concern is to rid ourselves of any and all dark spirits that challenge us. Should the opportunity to minister to someone else arise, we can then do so with confidence.

At the risk of being redundant, I must restate my conviction regarding the main intent of Matthew 10:1. It is a call for believers to wake up and take authority over the spirits that are oppressing them.

Do I Need Deliverance?

Oppressions and bondages are caused by dark spirits. The question is often asked, "How do I know if I have a problem that is caused by a spirit?" The answer will make some folks uncomfortable. The truth is if any area of your life is out of control, then you need to deal with an unclean spirit being in your life.

Believers should be aggressive or forceful in dealing with spirits of darkness. There are no successful "wimps" in the Kingdom of God.

Jesus tells us in Matthew 11:12 that the Kingdom of Heaven is under violent assault. Our Lord continued by declaring that only violent or forceful men lay hold on the Kingdom. The Kingdom is not a place; rather it is a state of being. It is the rule or reign of King Jesus in the heart of the believer.

The thrust of what Jesus is saying is that the rule of the King has and is being aggressively challenged by the forces of darkness. The battle will become more intense as the end of time draws nearer. The good news is that we, as believers, have been empowered with all the resources necessary to continue to be victorious.

The Meaning of Oppression

The reader should honestly acknowledge any area of his life that is out of control. Each area of oppression needs to be deliberately and willfully addressed.

It is extremely important to understand that some oppressions or bondages are not sinful. Some examples are fear, rejection and inferiority. Although these problems are not evil, they are none-the-less, emotionally and spiritually devastating.

Some examples of sinful bondage are anger, rage, lust, substance abuse, bitterness, resentment, unforgiveness and pornography. Possibilities are almost endless in this consideration.

No person is free to soar toward his or her destiny until becoming free from all bondages. A track and field runner can never approach his athletic potential if he runs with a sack of cement on his back. It is, likewise, imperative for every believer to deal with all bondages if he expects to embrace his destiny.

The believer who acknowledges the presence of bondage can be free. In I John 1:9, Jesus says, "If we confess our sins, He will be faithful and just to forgive us and cleanse us from all sin." This can be done right now, this very moment.

Perhaps the greatest hindrance in preparing for deliverance is the reticence and unwillingness to forgive those who have hurt or offended us. Jesus said that we cannot be forgiven unless we forgive the offending party.

Forgiving someone does not necessarily have to be an emotional choice. It can be done as an act of our will, along with an act of our faith. When we choose to forgive and pray, God will release us from bitterness and resentment.

An Exorcism Exercise

You may now be ready to begin involvement in this powerful ministry. It is imperative at this juncture that I point out that only folks who are sure of their salvation need to be involved at all. Continuing, I must again stress that all sins must be confessed up-to-date, and this absolutely must include deliberately letting go of all offences.

Deliverance is also a faith experience. Success in this ministry cannot be gauged by any certain feelings. Sometimes there are emotional responses or manifestations. None of these, however, are necessary for success. We do, as an act of faith, that which we sense God leading us to do, and we leave the result to Him.

The next order of business is to deal with the issues that we believe are present. If we do not know the identity of the troubling spirit or the name of the problem, God will reveal such to us as we pray. Some examples of these are fear, jealousy, anger, suicide, lust, rejection, inferiority. The possibilities are endless.

In the ministry of deliverance, I normally would follow the same routine or pattern. There were times when I deviated from my norm, but this did not happen often.

My normal mode of operation is to look right into the eyes of the person to whom I am ministering. Eyes have a way of being very revealing. I consider them to be windows of one's soul.

The procedure, I follow, is to call the spirit by name in a forceful manner, commanding them to leave in the name of Jesus Christ. Being forceful does not mean loudness, but rather confidence in assuming the authority given to us by our Lord.

Sometimes a spirit of darkness will actually argue with the one ministering. In such cases, it is necessary to be persistent and unruffled in declaring that their power is broken.

It is sometimes helpful to quote scripture and/or sing a song about the blood of Jesus in the process of this ministry. My wife and I have successfully assisted a countless number of precious people in their quest to be free.

There is an old saying that "one should clean up around his or her own doorstep" before admonishing another about their situation. Those interested in this ministry must have the honesty, courage and intestinal fortitude to forthrightly and successfully extricate all personal dark spirits.

One should only proceed to help others after taking care of the possible personal spirits in his own life. Ephesians 5:18 is pretty well a divine mandate for every form of ministry. This verse reads, "Be not drunk with wine wherein is excess; but be filled with the Holy Spirit." Success has everything to do with the Holy Spirit working in and through His ministers.

The term "be filled," is not a quantitative issue but rather a qualitative one. One who is drunk is under the influence of the substance which has been imbibed. The consequences are, therefore, undesirable, grievous and frequently devastating.

The Greek language verb structure in verse eighteen actually says, "being filled, be ye filled" with the Holy Spirit. It is quite obvious that our Lord is saying that His followers should, as a way of life, live under the influence of the Holy Spirit. This choice, too, must be a constant reality.

The result of this lifestyle is the only thing that will empower and equip the believer to minister effectively. Having settled this matter, one is ready for all divine appointments.

A word of caution is imperative here: Do not skulk around like a spiritual Sherlock Holmes expecting every troubled person to be a candidate for your exorcism. Be genuinely loving and caring about hurting people.

When word gets out that you really are the real deal as a minister of Jesus Christ, folks with problems of every description will flock to you. This includes people in need of exorcism or deliverance.

Be gentle with the wounded. Be careful in suggesting that people have a "demon." Desperate people will spill their insides to you. It will become clear quickly if they are under the control of an oppressive or dark spirit. If you offer them hope, they won't care what you name their problem. It is imperative that we respect the confidence of folks that are seeking help. If you live under the influence of the Holy Spirit, you indeed, are a candidate to help troubled individuals in this manner.

The Conclusion of this Matter

Be totally sold out to Jesus. You are powerless and can do nothing through your own resources. Living under the constant control of the Holy Spirit, you will soon be amazed at what He does through you.

Remember, Jesus Christ is everything that the Bible says He is. He still does everything that He ever did. You are everything that the Bible says you are. You can do everything that the Bible says that you can do.

Heed the admonition of William Carey when he said, "Attempt great things for God and expect great things from God." This will happen when we pray as the writer of the Book of Hebrews challenges: "Come to the throne of grace fearlessly, confidently and boldly."

Jesus declared that the harvest is plenteous, but the laborers are few; pray for the Lord of the harvest, that he will "thrust" forth laborers unto His harvest.

You are encouraged to take a moment and pray in the manner suggested above by the writer of the Book of Hebrews. As you do this, offer yourself to Him for whatever task that He may have in mind for you.

The Holy Spirit would have you to claim His words to the Apostle Paul as your very own: " I can do all things through Christ who pours His power into me." Incredible usefulness awaits those who will seize this word with abandon. Now is the time!

A Few Quirky Experiences to Make You Grin

The Bible says that "a merry heart doeth good like a medicine." It is a medical and scientific fact that laughter aids in the healing of the body. It is also beneficial to good mental and emotional health.

I learned early in life that if one can learn to laugh, the trip that we are on will be easier. The following stories are shared to help you to smile a bit today.

An Ancient Fable about an Apple

Billy Joe gave his heart to Jesus on a Sunday morning. It seems as though he had been religious for a long time but had never actually, as a choice of his will, received Jesus Christ into his heart. During the same altar call, his wife also came to renew her relationship with the Lord Jesus.

The next Sunday morning, Billy approached me with a very unusual proposition, "Pastor," he said, "Mary and I want you to baptize us in about three weeks. We want to be baptized at McIntosh landing on the Tombigbee River."

For a few moments, I was stunned and speechless at Billy's request. Recognizing my extremely puzzled expression, he quickly sought to explain himself. "Pastor, my fondest childhood memories are about the times I spent at McIntosh landing," he uttered in an almost muted voice. In this conversation, I learned that the trip to the baptismal site would be more than an hour's drive each way.

On the day of the trip, we left early enough to get back home by noon. My friends had one of those automobiles that are so small that once a person gets in, it's almost impossible for him to get out again. It was an ancient small Chevrolet of some kind and had only two doors. The only way to disembark from of one of those suckers is to literally crawl out.

The place of the baptismal rite was an ancient fishing village about seventy-fives miles north of Mobile, Alabama. The trip south was pleasant enough once I was settled in, what seemed like, an oversized infant's car seat.

As we traveled, Billy Joe rambled about his many delightful visits with his grandparents, and I silently prayed about the vast unknown that lay ahead of me that day. Each summer my friend declared that he would spend his days on his grandparents' houseboat doing nothing but fishing and swimming.

The once robust fishing community, I discovered, was now only a skeleton of what it once was. Not even a gasoline station or any other public facility was evident to us.

At this realization, I was almost overwhelmed with dismay. "Billy," I asked with a twinge of fear, "where will we change clothes after the baptism?"

"Heck fire, preacher, that won't be no problem," he declared with a smile a mile wide. "We'll just find a big 'ole bush; that's all we'll need."

Hit with this statement, I suddenly had a vision of the next day's edition of the Mobile Register Newspaper. On the front page, it read: "Mississippi pastor arrested for indecent exposure" at McIntosh Landing.

Things did not get any better after realizing that dire possibility. The water could not possibly have been more inappropriate in which to be immersed than it was that morning. The river was up about five feet. The water was a light brown color and was laden with all kinds of unsightly debris.

After the immersions were finished, I had a serious personal prayer time as I sought a bush large enough to keep me out of jail. Prayer again worked, and I changed clothes so quickly that it would have made Houdini proud.

After crawling back in the old Chevy, I began to feel somewhat self-righteous and smug. After all, I had made this long and disconcerting trip to serve my brother and to enhance and strengthen his childhood memories.

With a bit of pride, I asked, "Tell me again, Billy, why you wanted to be baptized at McIntosh Landing?" I fully expected him to launch into a monologue describing the awesome wonder of his childhood on a houseboat.

That was not his response at all. He did not hesitate for one second in his declaration. "Do you remember, preacher, the apple that Adam et when he fell away from God? Well, it was a McIntosh apple. That is really the reason that I wanted to be baptized at McIntosh Landing."

Devastated and totally crestfallen, all I could mutter was, "Oh." The entire rest of the trip homeward I languished in total silence and absolute abject despair and unbelief.

As time passed, Billy and I became good friends; and never once did I doubt the sincerity of his commitment to Jesus Christ. Unfortunately, several other incidents similar to the McIntosh apple episode surfaced over the years. To my disappointment, it became obvious that my friend marched to the tune of a different drummer.

World's Most Unusual Hymn

Joy and I were taking part in a spiritual emphasis week at a local nursing home. I was the speaker for this particular night, and Joy would be leading the singing. As we arrived at the meeting room, the patients were gathering for the service.

My wife and I entered the room as a quite elderly lady shuffled in with the aid of a walker. I greeted the lady and said that I was delighted she had come to the revival. She looked at me stoically. Attempting to cheer the sad lady with a bit of humor I said, "I would like for you to meet my Mother."

The lady suddenly brightened up and with a huge smile said, "I am so glad that you are not married."

Astonished at her response, I attempted to change the subject. I said, "Ma'am, you will really enjoy the singing tonight; what is your favorite hymn?"

"My favorite hymn is Kiss Me in the Moonlight," she responded jubilantly. The wisest and safest thing to do at this point was to stop talking and ask Joy to begin the music.

A Historical First

I came home laughing and feeling very smug. “Why are you laughing?” inquired my wife, Joy?

“I would have you know that I just did something that has never been done before. I creatively solved a problem, and I am quite pleased with myself,” I replied.

My Dad was living with us at that time, but health issues no longer allowed him to drive his car. I would occasionally drive the vehicle to keep the battery charged. On that particular day, I noticed that birds had roosted over the rear window and trunk of Dad’s car. It was one unsightly mess.

I decided to drive to the nearest carwash, while at the same time boost the battery’s power. I drove through the carwash and promptly got out to observe the results. I was absolutely frustrated at what I saw.

The washing mechanisms consisted of large brushes. These brushes moved along the sides of the vehicle, while another one rolled over the top of the car. I discovered that the big top brush just jumped over the back window. The window was untouched except for rivulets of water that sort of meandered down the glass. I had no inclination or intention of hand washing away several nights of bird droppings.

As I stared at the disgusting feathered flock’s layer of feces, it was like I experienced a miniature epiphany. An intuitive grasp of a simple and striking solution became crystal clear. I found myself in the joyful grip of my answer.

Smiling all the while, I drove Dad’s car back around to the entrance of the carwash. I was in possession of a rain check for that very carwash. I backed up to the entrance, got out and went to the other side and punched in the code to start the wash process. I proceeded to back the automobile into the washing position.

The rear window was now where the windshield normally would be. The big brush hovered over the problem area twice as the washing cycle ran its course. The result was a squeaky clean rear glass.

I laughed all the way through the story as I recounted it to my wife. I firmly assured her that most likely no one had ever accomplished this feat before. Unimpressed and obviously not sharing my pleasure, she simply shook her head and said, “I do hope that nobody saw you.”

Mistaken Identity

I was mortified and deeply embarrassed. I had just offended a very elderly retired pastor. He was ninety-five years old. He still drove his own car, bowled every week and seemed to be very alert.

I chanced to see him in a hallway in the Jeff Anderson Regional Medical Center. We greeted each other like the long-time friends that we were. After the initial greetings, I continued by asking how his wife was getting along.

His response hurt my heart deeply. "My wife died three years ago. How could you possibly have forgotten? You came to the funeral home to pay your respects."

My friend then added, "I just cannot believe that you have forgotten my wife's death." I was absolutely speechless. He then added, "Well, I have to go now. See you later, Bro. McElroy."

Epilogue

The passionate desire of this writer is to set your heart on fire with hope. If this happens, your best days definitely are yet to come.

This narrative is ending with good news for every reader. God's destiny for each one is two-fold. First, He wants you personally to experience miracles on an on-going basis.

Secondly, He desires for you to become a divine catalyst helping others to receive the miracle that they desperately need. Remember, it is not about what you are able to do; rather, it is about what the Holy Spirit can do through you.

You are encouraged to ask God for a divine appointment every day to minister to someone. Again, I stress that the Bible absolutely be taken at face value for your maximum effectiveness. It is also imperative that you deliberately embrace the truth that you really can do everything that the Bible says you can do.

The big question: Will you vigorously grasp this truth and run with it? Declare that you will, and begin now to implement this life changing truth. Your spirit will become pregnant with radiant and dynamic hope that will make the sky the limit for you.

Additional Books by this Author

Fascinating Miracles in the Life of a Country Preacher

This book is a record of some of the powerful and intriguing miracles in which this pastor has been involved. It is the conviction of this author that these captivating narratives will stir up a greater faith in all who read these accounts. Many who share in this exciting journey will become equipped to replicate similar miracles in their own lives.

Incredible Treasures Awaiting Discovery

This book is a compilation of carefully researched stories about buried or hidden treasure. Twenty one accounts of monetary treasure and two narratives of spiritual wealth are chronicled in this writing. The reader will be intrigued by the possibility of personally finding treasure. It is entirely possible that all who follow the directions in this manual will become incredibly wealthy. Paul Ott Carruth calls this a book a treasure map and Rev. Mike Boles declares it to be a "Masterpiece."

Unmasking Guerrilla Warfare in the Church

This book considers the seriousness of intolerance, bigotry, prejudice, and racism in the church of Jesus Christ. Jack Taylor, President of Dimension Ministries, declares, "This is a great story-line. It was so good that I read it through almost immediately. I am convinced that this book will be important to the church in the twenty-first century."

Dr. Fred Wolfe, Pastor Emeritus of Cottage Hill Baptist Church in Mobile, Alabama, says "I was greatly blessed by this book. The story is captivating and excellent reading. This powerful book is full of truth that must be heeded and obeyed. Read this book and go to war in the power of the cross. The time to act is now!"

Inquiries about these books may be made at: jackgiles1@bellsouth.net_or Jack O. Giles, 7387A State Boulevard Extension, Meridian, MS. 39305. Interested persons may also go online to www.authothouse.com and type in author's name in the appropriate place.

www.ingramcontent.com/pod-product-compliance
Ingram Content Group UK Ltd.
Pitfield, Milton Keynes, MK11 3LW, UK
UKHW040602210726
13854UKWH00008B/1713

9 781467 042772